C O L E

Your Guide to . . .

Scholarships and Bursaries

Funding for college & university

Province-by-province & Canada-wide lists

ABOUT COLES NOTES

COLES NOTES have been an indispensable aid to students on five continents since 1948.

COLES NOTES now offer titles on a wide range of general interest topics as well as traditional academic subject areas and individual literary works. All COLES NOTES are written by experts in their fields and reviewed for accuracy by independent authorities and the Coles Editorial Board.

COLES NOTES provide clear, concise explanations of their subject areas. Proper use of COLES NOTES will result in a broader understanding of the topic being studied. For academic subjects, COLES NOTES are an invaluable aid for study, review and exam preparation. For literary works, COLES NOTES provide interesting interpretations and evaluations which supplement the text but are not intended as a substitute for reading the text itself. Use of the NOTES will serve not only to clarify the material being studied, but should enhance the reader's enjoyment of the topic.

COLES PUBLISHING. A division of Prospero Books
Toronto - Canada
Printed in Canada

Cataloguing in Publication Data
Kidd, Darlene, 1948 -

Your guide to ... scholarships and bursaries

ISBN 0-7740-0618-8

1. Student aid - Canada - Directories.
2. Scholarships - Canada - Directories. I. Title. II. Series

LB2337.6.C35K52 1999 378.3'025'71 C99-931033-X

Publisher: Nigel Berrisford
Editing: Paul Kropp Communications
Book design: Karen Petherick, Markham, Ontario
Layout: Richard Hunt

Manufactured by Webcom Limited
Cover finish: Webcom's Exclusive DURACOAT

Contents

Introduction **Education, money and you** 1

Chapter 1 **Education: here's what it costs** 2
Typical budgets

Chapter 2 **Financial aid for university and college** 6
Loans
Bursaries
Scholarships
Grants
Fellowships
Awards
Part-time work

Chapter 3 **Across Canada – federal and provincial loans** 8
Canada student loans program
Provincial loans
Alberta
British Columbia
Manitoba
New Brunswick
Newfoundland
Northwest Territories
Nova Scotia
Prince Edward Island
Ontario
Quebec
Saskatchewan
Yukon

Chapter 4 **Across Canada – scholarships and bursaries** 24

Chapter 5 **Provincial scholarship information** 26

Chapter 6 **Provincial scholarships** 29
Federal awards
Alberta
British Columbia
Manitoba
New Brunswick

Newfoundland
Northwest Territories
Nova Scotia
Ontario
Prince Edward Island
Quebec
Saskatchewan
Federal-provincial programs

Chapter 7 **Private foundations and corporations** 45

Chapter 8 **Armed forces awards/scholarships** 57

Chapter 9 **Athletic awards** 61

Chapter 10 **Scholarships for specific groups** 65
First Nations Canadians
Visible minorities
Students with physical and learning disabilities
International students
Corporate scholarships

Chapter 11 **American scholarships** 74

Chapter 12 **Preparing to win the scholarship** 76
Frequenly asked questions
Nothing breeds success like success

Chapter 13 **Worksheets** 85
Student worksheet
Aids to help you apply for scholarships
Parent worksheet
Scholarship coach worksheet

Chapter 14 **Sample questions from scholarship applications** 94

Chapter 15 **How to help someone write a reference for you** 102
Sample letters of reference
Student involvement checklist

Chapter 16 **Your personal history** 108
Work history
Academic history
Addresses and telephone numbers

Education, money and you

Most students are unaware of how much funding is available for post-secondary education. Governments, the corporate sector and public-service organizations all provide funding for prospective students - loans, bursaries, grants, fellowships, awards and scholarships. In fact, local, provincial and national agencies offer thousands of loans, bursaries and scholarships to Canadian post-secondary students. This information is not a closely guarded secret. Information regarding the availability of this funding is readily available in many libraries and schools. However, the sheer volume of information is intimidating. It is rarely stored in an organized or accessible fashion, the information may be available without the proper instructions or application form and the criteria is often confusing. Even if students become aware of some avenues of financial aid, often they still do not apply. Whatever the reason, you can miss out on available and valuable financial resources.

This book will let you know what's available and how to apply for financial aid for your post-secondary education. Many students don't realize that applying for financial aid requires work. And work starts early. That means that if you are planning to enter a post-secondary institution you need to begin your research on possible funding as soon as possible. Grade 9 or 10 is not too early.

If you're successful in your scholarship search - and almost any student can be - much of your post-secondary education will be paid for by someone besides you and your parents. All you need is the confidence and determination to seek out the help you need.

CHAPTER ONE

Education: here's what it costs

Education has always carried a price tag. From the earliest formalized education, Plato and Aristotle mentored students in exchange for trade goods and domestic service. Monks taught young men the wonders of mathematics and astrology in exchange for cleaning and cooking services in the monastery. Master tradespeople supervised young apprentices for a period of several years – welders, jewellers, blacksmiths, hairdressers, seamstresses, milliners, wheelwrights – and modern apprenticeships differ only in the terms that are set.

Although the price of education has always been high, it used to be possible to save enough for the following year's tuition by taking a low-paying summer job and living at home. Unfortunately, even well-paying summer jobs seldom cover the tuition costs of today. Tuition costs at Canadian universities continue to rise at rates far beyond inflation. Couple that with the increased costs of housing, transportation, books and clothing for most students living away from home and you have an extremely expensive education.

The common adage says that an education is priceless. While this is true, the *costs* of getting that education are driven forever upwards by reduced government grants for education. In the last generation, the dollar cost of tuition alone has increased tenfold.

From all indicators, education will continue to cost more. Books and paper will become more expensive, wages will continue to spiral and governments, while giving lip-service to the importance and need for education, will continue to reduce their spending on post-secondary training. There may be temporary exceptions to this trend (especially if you belong to certain ethnic groups or pursue training in a certain field where there is a shortage of trained personnel), but the trend will continue.

These sobering statistics lead students considering post-secondary education to research their scholarship, bursary and student loan options. Where entrance averages and the choice of programs and institutions have traditionally been the major concern of prospective students, now the focus may well have turned to finances.

Typical budget for Canadian university student, year 2000

Income		
Savings		$2,000
High-school scholarships		
Employers' scholarships		
Entrance scholarships		750
Loans		2,000
Bursaries		
Part-time or summer employment income		2,000
Parental contributions		2,000
Total income		8,750
Expenses		
Tuition		3,200
Books & supplies		500
Dormitory	($250/mo. x 8)	2,000
Food		2,000
Recreation		600
Clothing		600
Local transportation	($50 x 6)	300
Long-range transportation	($50 X 4)	200
Telephone		400
Miscellaneous		100
Total expenses		$9,900

Typical budget for community college student, year 2000

Income		
Savings		2,000
High-school scholarships		
Employers' scholarships		
Entrance scholarships		500
Loans		1,500
Bursaries		
Part-time employment income		1,600
Parental contributions		2,000
Total income		7,600
Expenses		
Tuition		2,500
Books & supplies		850
Residence	($252/mo. x 8)	2,016
Food		640
Recreation		400
Transportation		400
Telephone		400
Miscellaneous		200
Total expenses		$7,406

Most of this book will show you how to add money to the scholarship and bursary lines in your college or university budget, but it would be wise to consider other ways to get the income and expenses in balance.

Savings The more you save in high school, the easier it will be to finance your post-secondary education. Even relatively poor-paying jobs such as babysitting, part-time work in department stores or pumping gasoline can be a definite asset. You will likely have little or no financial responsibility while you live at home, so this is an excellent opportunity to save and at the same time learn to budget. Money-management skills are a definite plus to have when you enter post-secondary training.

Part-time work Many universities and colleges make this available to students who wish to make a little extra cash to help pay their way through college. Part-time work may be on or off campus. If it is limited to few-enough hours to not interfere with classes or studying, it can help balance the annual budget.

Dormitory/housing Yes, you can save money by living at home (probably $4,000 a year), but you'll likely spend more on transportation and entertainment.

Parental contribution Not all parents can kick in for post-secondary education, but it doesn't hurt to ask. There are good arguments on your side. For one, if you're off at school, you don't have to be fed (a saving of a good $1,000 a year). For another, most colleges and universities expect that parents will provide some money when they calculate your scholarship award. Finally, you can sometimes transfer the income-tax deduction for tuition fees to your parents - this will give them a tax saving.

- Education is pricey.
- Financial help is available.
- *You* deserve to get that help.
- This book will show you how.

CHAPTER TWO

Financial aid for university and college

There is more financial aid available to Canadian students than ever before. However, getting that assistance requires much work, beginning with the awareness of the available options and programs. Some financial assistance alternatives include loans, bursaries, scholarships, grants, fellowships, awards and part-time work. Let's consider each of these.

LOANS

Loans are administered by governments for the purpose of financing your education. They are usually interest-free as long as you are enrolled at a post-secondary institution. Most provincial loans continue to be interest-free for six months after you graduate or terminate your studies. By that date, the borrower may choose to repay the entire loan or begin to make payments that include repayment of the principal of the loan plus interest. Students - not their parents - must apply for loans.

BURSARIES

Bursaries are funding for education based on academic achievement and financial need. These are offered by universities or colleges, governments, corporations or service organizations. Students are not required to repay the amount of the bursary, but often must reapply for the bursary each year.

SCHOLARSHIPS

Scholarships are awarded to students based on academic achievement, extracurricular activities, athletic ability or community service. Sources include governments, post-secondary institutions, corporations and community service organizations. Students are not required to repay scholarships, but must apply for them and continue to meet the scholarship requirements for their entire post-secondary career.

GRANTS

Grants are given to eligible students who demonstrate financial need or meet other criteria. Grants are non-repayable, but must be applied for by the student.

FELLOWSHIPS

Fellowships are awarded to full-time doctoral students based on academic excellence.

AWARDS

Awards are free money granted to eligible students usually on the basis of academic or other criteria. You are usually granted an award without applying for it, often on graduation.

PART-TIME WORK

Many students choose to finance their post-secondary training by doing part-time work. Some take less than a full course load of classes each year and consequently take longer to complete their post-secondary schooling because they choose to graduate with little debt, essentially working their way through school. Some universities arrange for 10-15 hours a week of part-time work for students who receive financial aid. This ordinarily does not interfere with studies or extend the degree program, and it can provide $3,000 a year or more towards your budget. Many students arrange for similar work (waiting tables, bartending, etc.) on their own.

Co-op students, who are placed in work terms as part of their program, find that co-op job payments are often sufficient to pay for the next semester back at university or college.

CHAPTER THREE

Across Canada – federal and provincial loans

CANADA STUDENT LOANS PROGRAM

According to the current brochure *Canada Student Loans Program, Financing Your Post-Secondary Education*, "… federal and provincial governments provide financial assistance (loans or non-repayable grants) to eligible students based on their demonstrated financial need. In the nine provinces and Yukon that participate in the federal Canada Student Loans Program (CSLP), needy students may receive both federal and provincial assistance although they apply using one form. Quebec and Northwest Territories have opted out of the CSLP and receive compensation from the federal government towards the costs of their own student assistance program."

The cost of your studies as well as your resources are considered when you apply for a loan. Your earnings during the four months previous to returning to post-secondary school are figured in. Canada student loans are provided for up to 60 percent of your assessed financial need up to a weekly loan limit (currently $165) for full-time students. Part-time students may receive loans in proportion to their costs. Each province decides how much financial assistance to contribute on top of the federal loan.

The Canada Student Loans Program also administers Canada study grants for:

- high-need part-time students
- students with permanent disabilities
- women in doctoral studies
- students with dependents

For a more detailed listing of the above information contact:

Learning Directorate
Human Resources Development Canada
P.O. Box 2090, Station D
Ottawa ON K1P 6C6
Internet: www.hrdc-drhc.gc.ca/student_loans

or

Enquiries Centre
Human Resources Development Canada
140 promenade du Portage
Phase IV, Level O
Hull PQ K1A 0J9
Internet: www.hrdc-drhc.gc.ca

or

your provincial address for student loans (listed later)

It is your responsibility to contact the bank or credit union each year to ensure that the interest-free status of both the Canadian and provincial student loans is continued or reinstated while you are in school. Canada student loans begin to accrue interest on the first day of the first month after your study period is concluded. Payments must begin six months after the study period ends and it is your responsibility to have made arrangements for a payment schedule before that time has passed.

How terrible is student debt?

Many students finish their university careers carrying a debt of $20,000 or $25,000 or more … which sounds like an awful lot of debt when there's no guarantee of a job after your schooling is finished. On the other hand, that much money is about as much as you'd be in debt if you purchased a mid-sized car. After ten years your car will be rusted – but your education will still be paying off.

1. Apply for a loan if you think you qualify and need the funds.
2. Apply early.
3. Ask for only what you need!
4. Contact the address supplied for your province/territory to ensure that you receive the most current guidelines and eligibility information. These conditions change frequently.
5. You may pay down your student loan anytime without a penalty.
6. The longer you take to repay your loan, the more interest you will eventually pay.

PROVINCIAL LOANS

Alberta

Alberta student loans are administered by the Students' Finance Board which handles the Alberta and Canada Student Loans programs. Some part of the awarded assistance may be designated as a non-repayable grant or bursary. Alberta students who can prove financial need and are enrolled in at least 60 percent of a full course load are eligible for some loan and grant assistance. Federal and provincial loans are interest-free for the study period and the provincial loan is interest-free for six months following that period.

Applications and full details are available from the financial assistance office of post-secondary schools or all Alberta Career Development Centres. Contact the center nearest you, listed in the telephone directory, or:

Canada/Alberta Service Centre
Henry Hayes Building, Room 280
220-4th Ave. SE
Calgary AB T2G 4X3
Internet: www.alberta-learning.ab.ca

Canada Place
Canada/Alberta
Service Centre
9700 Jasper Ave.
Edmonton AB T4V 4E2

Available programs:

1. Canada Student Loan
2. Alberta Student Loan

- Commercial Flight Training Loan. Up to $4,900 per flight component or up to $19,600 is available to students to complete four components of fixed wing training or an entire helicopter program. Private pilot license or the completion of build-up time are exempt.
- Alberta Opportunities Bursary. This is for students who have an assessed need greater than $4,000 in their first or second year of post-secondary training.
- Northern Student Supplement. This bursary is for students who qualify for the Alberta Opportunities Bursary and are from Northern Alberta.

3. Canada Study Grant. The federal government has introduced a new grant program to assist high-need students, with children or other dependents, whose needs are not met through scholarship and student loans.
4. Grants for full-time students in upgrading/basic foundation skills programs. Financially disadvantaged adults who are unemployed and unskilled may be eligible to receive funding to enable them to take academic upgrading; adult basic education; literacy and numeracy; English as a second language; pre-careers academic preparation training; pre-technology training or university and college entrance preparation.
5. Labour Market Programs. To be eligible for student assistance, a student must be eligible to receive Employment Insurance Benefits.

British Columbia

British Columbia Student Assistance Program (BCSAP) is open to British Columbia residents who require assistance to finance their education. This assistance takes the form of a federal Canada student loan combined with a British Columbia student loan to a possible maximum of $260/week for the duration of the study period. Loans must be repaid beginning six months after the completion of your study period, regardless of whether you have successfully completed the course. The government will have covered the interest payments while you are in school and during the regular summer recesses; after graduation, the interest buildup must be paid off by you.

Application forms and information regarding the most recent details of the British Columbia Student Assistance Program are available from the post-secondary school financial assistance offices or:

Students Services Branch
Ministry of Advanced Education, Training and Technology
2nd Floor, 1106 Cook St.
Victoria BC V8V 3Z9
Internet: www.dett.gov.bc.ca/studentservices

Mailing address:

P.O. Box 9173
Station Provincial Government
Victoria BC V8W 9H7

Available programs:

1. Canada Student Loan
2. British Columbia Student Loan
3. British Columbia Grant. This is available to high-need students enrolled in their first 68 weeks of full-time post-secondary study. High-need students are those whose assessed need is in excess of $105/week of study. Students are expected to use their Canada student loan and British Columbia student loan first. They are not required to repay their British Columbia grant unless there was an overaward, or students withdraw from their educational program or do not use loan money first.
4. Loan Remission. If the total value of all loans surpasses a certain level after the completion of a certificate, diploma or degree, you may be granted a loan remission, which would be applied towards the outstanding British Columbia loan only.
5. Adult Basic Education Student Assistance Program
6. Student Society Emergency Aid Fund. This helps students in a financial crisis who would need to postpone their studies at a British Columbia post-secondary school.

7. Work Study. Supplemental work opportunities are supplied for students who have exhausted the British Columbia Student Assistance Program as a resource, but are still in need.
8. Canada Study Grant for Students with Permanent Disabilitiies
9. Canada Study Grant for High-Need Part-Time Students
10. Canada Study Grant for Female Doctoral Students
11. Canada Study Grant for Students with Disabilities

Each province has its own form for applying for a student loan, but here's what almost all of them require:

- your name, address, social insurance number, sex and date of birth
- your parents' name(s), address(es), place(s) of employment (if your parents are divorced, you still have to list both)
- any income you have
- the income(s) of your custodial parent(s)

Manitoba

Canada Student Loans and Manitoba Government Loans/ Grants are available by applying on one form and submitting that application to the Student Financial Assistance Office. Canadian Student Loans are granted first with Manitoba Government Loans/ Grants supplementing students whose needs exceeds what is available from Canada Student Loans. Manitoba Study Assistance is an additional amount available to students whose need exceeds the maximum allowance from Canada and Manitoba Student Loans. Repayment of both loans must begin six months after the end of your final study period. Manitoba pays the interest on the loan for the first six-month period, whereas the Canada loan will begin to accrue interest on the first day of the first month after the completion of your study period.

Application forms and details concerning the Canada and Manitoba Student Loans programs are available from:

Manitoba Education and Training
Student Financial Assistance Office
P.O. Box 6
693 Taylor Ave.
Winnipeg MB R3M 3T9

Available programs:

1. Canada Student Loan
2. Manitoba Student Loan
3. Manitoba Study Assistance. This is a non-repayable grant for students who have exhausted all other support sources and have needs exceeding the maximum Canada Student Loan and Manitoba Student Loan amounts (up to $40/week for the study period).
4. Prince of Wales/Princess Anne Award. To be eligible for this non-repayable assistance, students must have a need as determined on the Canada Student Loan/Manitoba Student Loan Assessment (up to $200/year).
5. Canada Student Loan for Part-Time Students (up to $4,000/year).
6. Canada Study Grant for High-Need Part-Time Students (up to $1,200/year).
7. Canada Study Grant for Students with Permanent Disabilities (up to $3,000/year).
8. Canada Study Grant for Female Doctoral Students (up to $3,000/year for three years).

New Brunswick

New Brunswick operates a combined New Brunswick Student Loan/Canada Student Loan Program. The eligibility is similar to that of other provinces except that students must be enrolled in a minimum of 80 percent of a full-time course load at a New Brunswick post-secondary school (or an educational institution outside the province only if that particular course of study is not offered in the province). The Canada student loan is available to cover 60 percent of the assessed need up to a maximum of $165/week of the study period, while the New Brunswick student loan will cover an additional 40 percent of the assessed need to a maximum of $110/week. Repayment of the loans must begin six months after the study period ends. Although interest begins to accrue on the New Brunswick portion of the loan at the six-month mark, the interest on the Canada student loan will have begun to accrue on the first day of the first month following the termination of the study period.

For detailed information regarding student financial assistance and application forms, contact:

Student Services Branch
Department of Education
P.O. Box 6000
548 York St.
Fredericton NB E3B 5H1
E-mail: finpostsec@gov.nb.ca
Internet: www.gov.nb.ca/ael/strasse.htm

Available programs:

1. Canada Student Loan
2. New Brunswick Student Loan
3. New Brunswick Bursary. To be eligible, the student's need must exceed the maximum provincial and federal loans available.
4. Canada Student Loan for Part-Time Study
5. Assistance for High-Need Part-Time Students
6. New Brunswick Women's Doctoral Scholarship Program
7. Canada Study Grant for Female Doctoral Students

Newfoundland

Both the Canada and Newfoundland/Labrador Student Loans Programs are administered by the Division of Student Aid in the Department of Education and are similar in many respects. Both are needs-based and intended to supplement the resources of students and their familites. The Canada Student Loans Program will provide assistance to a maximum of 60 percent of the assessed need up to $165/week of study. The Newfoundland Student Loans Program will supply the remaining 40 percent of assessed need to a maximum of $110/week of study. Students must be enrolled in a full-time program taking a minimum of a 60 percent course load. All Canada and Newfoundland student loans must be repaid with interest upon graduation or termination of studies. While you are given a six month grace period before you are required to consolidate your student loans and begin repayment, interest begins to accrue as of *end date of the period of study* shown on the student's Canada and Newfoundland Student Loan Certificates.

For detailed information regarding student financial assistance and application procedures, contact:

Student Aid Division
Department of Education
Thompson Student Centre
P.O. Box 8700, 3rd Floor
St. John's NF A1B 4J6
E-mail: student@aid.gov.nf.ca
Internet: www.edu.gov.nf.ca/studentaid/

Available programs:

1. Canada Student Loan
2. Newfoundland Student Loan
3. Canada Study Grant for High-Need Part-Time Students
4. Canada Study Grant for Persons with Permanent Disabilities
5. Canada Study Grant for Female Doctoral Students
6. Loan Remission Program. This is a form of loan forgiveness that is applicable if the combined Canada and Newfoundland student loan debt exceeds the minimum debt threshold as defined in the Student Aid Program application form.
7. Interest Relief Program. There is both a Canada Student Loans Interest Relief Plan and a Newfoundland Student Loans Interest Relief Program. Applicants who meet the eligibility criteria are not required to make principal or interest payments on their loans during the approved interest relief period. This relief is usually granted for three-month periods for a maximum lifetime benefit of 30 months during the first five years for Canada student loans and for a maximum lifetime benefit of 18 months within the first three years for Newfoundland student loans.

Northwest Territories

Northwest Territories administers a student financial assistance program independent of the Canada Student Loans Program. Canadian citizens who have been accepted at an approved institution as full-time post-secondary students and have been NWT residents for at least one year are eligible. Applications must be made by July 15. Repayment of loans must begin six months after the study period ends. Failure to negotiate a repayment schedule within six months of the end of the study period results in the total loan plus accrued interest becoming payable seven months after the study period ends. For details and application forms, contact:

Student Services
Department of Education, Culture and Employment
P.O. Box 1320
Yellowknife NT X1A 2L9

Available programs:

1. Basic Grants. These support travel and tuition to NWT students.
2. Supplementary Grants. These provide additional funds to aboriginal students enrolled in post-secondary studies.
3. NWT Student Loan. Students are entitled to funds to cover one academic year for every three years of residence in NWT. In addition to the basic grant, students may borrow up to $3,200/ year.
4. Correspondence Course Reimbursement. The department will reimburse students who have successfully completed post-secondary correspondence courses up to $250/course.
5. Loan Remission. Students who have successfully completed 60 percent of their training and returned to the NWT to live may be excused from repaying part or all of their primary loan.

Nova Scotia

The Nova Scotia government along with the Canadian government offer student loans to post-secondary students of Nova Scotia. The Canada Student Loans Program provides funding for 60 percent of the assessed need to a maximum of $165/week of the study period while Nova Scotia Student Loans supply 40 percent to a maximum of $150/week of study period. Students in Nova Scotia are considered to be full-time students if they are taking at least 60 percent of a full course load. You will be required to begin repayment six months after the date shown on the loan document as of the end of the study period. Interest on the provincial portion of the loan will begin to accrue at this time, while the interest on the Canada student loan begins to accrue immediately upon completion of the study period.

For detailed information regarding student financial assistance and application forms, contact:

Student Assistance Office
Department of Education and Culture
P.O. Box 2290, Halifax Central
Halifax NS B3J 3C8
E-mail: stuasst@gov.ns.ca
Internet: www.ednet.ns.ca/educ/student

Available programs:

1. Canada Student Loan
2. Nova Scotia Student Loan
3. Loan Remission
4. Canada Study Grant for High-Need Part-Time Students
5. Canada Study Grant for Students with Disabilities
6. Canada Study Grant for Women in Doctoral Studies

Ontario

When students apply to the Ontario Student Assistance Program, they automatically make application for a Canada student loan and/or an Ontario student loan. OSAP requires that a student is a Canadian resident, an Ontario resident and is enrolled in an approved post-secondary program. Students will be expected to enroll in at least 60 percent of a full course load; students with disabilitiies must be enrolled in at least 40 percent of a full course load. Post-secondary programs must be at least four weeks in length to qualify.

There's a new wrinkle - if you are applying for a loan for the first time in 1998-99 or later, the ministry will perform a credit check. You will not be eligible for an Ontario student loan if you are more than 90 days in arrears on three or more personal loans or credit accounts, each with a value of $1,000 or more.

The federal and provincial governments will cover the interest charges of your loans while you are in school. Interest begins to accrue on both loans on the first day of the first month after the study period ends. It is suggested that application to OSAP be made by June 30 of the applicable year.

For detailed information or application forms, contact:

Student Support Branch
Ministry of Education and Training
P.O. Box 4500
189 Red River Rd., 4th Floor
Thunder Bay ON P7B 6G9
Internet: OSAP. gov.on.ca

Available programs:

1. Canada Student Loan
2. Part-Time Canada Student Loans Program
3. Canada Study Grants for Female Doctoral Students
4. Canada Study Grants for High-Need Part-Time Students
5. Ontario Student Loans Plan
6. Ontario Special Bursary Plan
7. Bursary for Students with Disabilities
8. Ontario Work Study Plan
9. Child-Care Bursary Plan
10. Loan Forgiveness Program
11. Interest Relief Program

When you're on your own

Parental income is a key factor in determining financial aid for students just out of high school, but what does it take to be an "independent" student? In most provinces, you need to have been out of seconday school for 48 months or have been in the workforce for two periods of 12 consecutive months each to qualify. If you meet the criteria, then only *your* income is considered when you apply for financial aid.

Prince Edward Island

The Prince Edward Island government administers a student loan program in conjunction with the Government of Canada. The Canada Student Loans Program will provide assistance for 60 percent of the assessed student need to a maximum of $165/week of the study period, while Prince Edward Island Student Loans will supply the remaining 40 percent to a maximum of $110/week of study. Canadian students who are P.E.I. residents are eligible for loan assistance if they can demonstrate their available funds are insufficient to finance their education and living costs while they are enrolled as full-time students at a post-secondary institution designated by P.E.I.

Your course must be of at least 12 weeks duration and a student must enroll in at least 60 percent of a full-time course load. You must begin repayment of the provincial loan six months after the study period ends. Provincial interest will be applied only then. Repayment of your Canada student loan may also be deferred until six months after the study period ends, but interest will be charged starting the first day of the first month after the study period ends. Application for financial assistance should be made by July 1.

Applications forms and more detailed information can be obtained from:

Student Financial Services
Department of Education
P.O. Box 2000
105 Rochford St.
Shaw Building, 3rd Floor
Charlottetown PE C1A 7N8
E-mail: studentloan@gov.pe.ca
Internet: www.ael.gov.nb.ca/staappl/saapplic.htm

Available programs:

1. Canada Student Loan
2. Prince Edward Island Student Loan
3. Prince Edward Island Debt Reduction Grant
4. Canada Study Grant for High-Need Part-Time Study
5. Canada Study Grant for Students with Disabilities
6. Canada Study Grant for Women in Doctoral Studies

Quebec

Quebec Student Assistance Plan operates separately from those of the other provinces and territories. Government aid is offered as guaranteed loans or as a combination of loans and bursaries. Advance loans of $500 to single students or $775 to students with dependents may be issued at the time of application to those in a situation that may lead to total destitution. Repayment of the loan must begin six months after the end of the study period, but interest will begin to accrue on the loan the first day of the first month after the study period. Depending on the program taken, students are assessed an overall debt limit for their studies. It is suggested that any application for student financial aid be submitted by June 30.

For further details and application forms, contact:

Direction générale de l'aide financière aux étudiants
Ministère de l'Éducation
1035 rue de la Chevrotiere
Québec PQ G1R 5A5
Internet: www.meq.gouv.qc.ca/afe

Available programs:

1. Student Loans
2. Student Bursaries. If you are attending an educational institution designated for both loans and busaries and have been awarded the maximum loan but it does not cover all allowable expenses, you will automatically qualify for a bursary. In 1998 the maximum student loan, depending on the program enrolled in, was $6,000 per term while the maximum bursary was $11,255.

Saskatchewan

Saskatchewan student loans are administered by the Student Financial Assistance Unit that handles Saskatchewan and Canada Student Loans. Loans are available for study outside of the province depending on your reason for attending a particular institution. The combined provincial and federal loan amount depends on the difference between your estimated assets and projected living and study expenses including tuition, books, transportation and rent. In

1998 a regular single student received funding for up to $275/week with a debt reduction level of $95/week. You are expected to work during the four-month pre-study term and your parents are expected to make some contribution to your expenses, unless you have been living away from home for four years or have been in the work-force for two periods of 12 consecutive months since leaving school.

Applications and detailed information are available from the financial assistance offices of post-secondary institutions, as well as:

> Student Financial Assistance Unit
> Saskatchewan Post-Secondary Education and Skills Training
> Room B21, Walter Scott Building
> 3085 Albert St.
> Regina SK S4P 3V5

Available programs:

1. Canada Student Loan
2. Saskatchewan Student Loan
3. Saskatchewan Student Bursary. This will equal the full amount of your assistance (loan) that exceeds $180/week of study period.
4. Canada and Saskatchewan Study Grants. These are available to students with dependent children and those whose loan assistance exceeds $275/week of study period.
5. Remission. This is available to Special Incentive Students (single parents, non-status Indians/Metis and/or Northerners) for the first 60 weeks of post-secondary study and those whose student loan assistance exceeds $105/week of study period.
6. Canada Study Grant (for full-time and part-time students)
7. Permanent Disability Benefit (loan forgiveness)
8. Employability Assistance for People with Disabilities
9. Full-Time Students Taking Short Courses
10. Canada Study Grant for Part-Time Students
11. Canada Study Grant for Female Doctoral Students

Yukon

The Yukon administers a Canada and Yukon student financial assistance program. Students who are less than 19 years of age and have resided and attended school in the Yukon are eligible to apply for assistance. The Yukon grant does not have to be repaid unless you withdraw from classes or drop to a part-time status, in which case you will be required to pay back a portion of the grant within three months. No repayment of the student training allowance is required.

For details and an application form, contact:

Students Financial Assistance Unit
Advanced Education Branch
Department of Education
P.O. Box 2703
Whitehorse YT Y1A 2C6
E-mail: carole.theriault@gov.yk.ca
Internet: www.yesnet.yk.ca/sites/sfa

Available programs:

1. Canada Student Loan
2. Yukon Grant
3. Student Training Allowance
4. Yukon Excellence Awards
5. Canada Study Grant for Students with Permanent Disabilities
6. Canada Study Grant for Women in Doctoral Studies
7. Canada Study Grant for Part-Time Students

CHAPTER FOUR

Across Canada – scholarships and bursaries

You should always take a systematic approach to discovering what is available in the line of financial assistance, beginning with research into what opportunities exist at the local, provincial, national and, finally, international level.

Be alert to scholarship and bursary opportunities offered within the immediate community. It is helpful to watch newspaper reports of present winners and scholarship/bursary opportunities for at least two or three years before you are eligible to apply. Scholarship/bursary guidelines and winners are often displayed at the local high school. Your school guidance counsellor should be able to supply a list of locally available scholarships, bursaries and awards. Another avenue is to query local clubs and organizations regarding scholarship opportunities they offer.

Most provincial and territorial departments of education have compiled lists of available scholarships, bursaries and awards for their jurisdiction. Certainly each of the post-secondary institutions have collated lists of scholarships, bursaries, awards and loans for which their prospective students are eligible.

Several sources of information are available at the national level outlining available student financial assistance. In addition to the publications listed in chapter 3 regarding student loans, two other publications are very helpful and regularly revised - most major libraries have copies of the *Canadian Directory of Foundations and Granting Agencies Sources of Funds Index* and the awards publication of the Association of Universities and Colleges of Canada (AUCC). If these two publications are not available at your local library, they can be ordered through interlibrary loan. Check with the librarian.

The Internet can also be helpful in locating scholarship opportunities. One address to try is: www.fastweb.com/canada. This Web site allows students to enter their personal information and establish an address where their file can be updated with available scholarships regularly.

Information regarding study and financial assistance at post-secondary institutions outside Canada should be available at the student financial assistance office at any college or university you wish to attend in the United States or overseas. It may be necessary to write to the intended college of study to receive detailed information. A search for scholarships on the Internet reveals that there are over 9,000 available Web sites for American scholarships alone.

Some of the scholarship "opportunities" publicized on the Internet are nothing more than scams to grab your money for "application fees" or other costs - with no real scholarship in the future. Always write for confirming information or check with your school guidance counsellor; be sceptical of such offers. If a deal sounds too good to be true, it probably is. Remember, if you are asked to pay money to qualify for a scholarship, it is a scam.

CHAPTER FIVE

Provincial scholarship information

Unless this book were revised and reprinted several times a year, any list of available scholarships and bursaries would be out of date by the time of publication. Even when the job of collating the hundreds of scholarships and bursaries for each province is "done," it is rarely complete. There are just too many sources for you to do a thorough search and become aware of every scholarship in the province or territory at any one time.

The following departments of education have indicated that they do keep a file of most of the current scholarships for their province and supply that list to schools. We suggest that you contact the appropriate provincial and territorial agency to ensure that your list of scholarship opportunities is the most current and correct.

Achieving Excellence
The Alberta Heritage Scholarship Fund
Alberta Advanced Education and Career Development
Commerce Place, 101155-102 St.
Edmonton AB T5J 4L5

Learning Resources Branch
Ministry of Education
Parliament Buildings
Victoria BC V8V 1X8
Ask for: *Financial Opportunities for Students*

Department of Education and Training
Manager of High School Certification
Evaluation, Research and Planning Division
Government of Newfoundland and Labrador
P.O. Box 8700
St. John's NF A1B 4J8

David Gilday, Director, Career Development
NWT Education, Culture and Employment
Government of Northwest Territories X1A 2L9

The Loans and Bursaries Program
Student Financial Assistance
Ministère de l'éducation
Édifice Marie-Guyart
11th Étage
1035 rue de la Chevrotiere
Québec PQ G1R 5A5

Student Financial Assistance Unit
Saskatchewan Post Secondary Education and Skills Training
Room B21, Walter Scott Building
3085 Albert St.
Regina SK S4P 3V7
(A comprehensive list of 450 scholarships and bursaries available to Saskatchewan students is printed by this department annually.)

Student Financial Assistance
Department of Education
Government of Yukon
P.O. Box 2703
Whitehorse YT Y1A 2C6

Here are the addresses for the remainder of the departments that responded. They may or may not have a collated list of the scholarships available to students in their provinces when you're ready to apply.

Manitoba Department of Education and Training
Student Financial Assistance
409-1181 Portage Ave.
Winnipeg MB R3G 0T3

New Brunswick Educational Services Division
440 King St.
King's Place
Fredericton NB E3B 5H1

Nova Scotia Department of Education and Culture
P.O. Box 2290
Halifax Central
Halifax NS B3J 3C8

Prince Edward Island Office of Education
Shaw Building
105 Rochford St., 3rd Floor,
P.O. Box 2000
Charlottetown PE C1A 7N8

Ontario Ministry of Education and Training
Mowat Block, 900 Bay St.
Toronto ON M7A 1L2

CHAPTER SIX

Provincial scholarships

FEDERAL AWARDS

1. **Governor-General's Bronze Medal Awards** are provided to the student with the highest academic average in each post-secondary school in Canada. That student's average must be 80 percent or higher.
2. **The Canada Millennium Scholarships** are available to low- and middle-income post-secondary students enrolled in programs at publicly funded post-secondary institutions. There should be approximately 100,000 scholarships averaging $3,000 annually. These will be awarded on the basis of financial need and merit.
3. **The Canada Education Savings Grant (CESG),** is not exactly a scholarship, but a special bonus if your parents have put money away for you in an RESP. The federal government will provide the equivalent to 20 percent of the first $2,000 of the Registered Education Savings Plan contribution, to be paid into any RESP. The investment income earned on the savings as well as the grant payments will be sheltered from tax until the student uses the money to finance costs of learning. Funds can be moved between siblings. However, if a student does not pursue higher education within a reasonable period of time, the grant will have to be repaid.

RESPs

RESPs (Registered Education Savings Plans) offer families a tax break and a financial bonus if they manage to save for their kids' post-secondary educations. More than a million parents and grandparents contribute to an RESP every year. The government offers a cash bonus of 20 percent of the RESP contribution up to $400, and your parents don't have to pay any tax on the money saved (though you do, when you draw on the money to use for college or university). If your family had put $50 a month into an RESP starting 15 years ago, you'd have almost $20,000 set aside today for your tuition and expenses.

ALBERTA

Enquiries about all Alberta scholarships should be directed to Alberta Heritage Scholarship Fund Office, 9th Floor, 9940 106 St., P.O. Box 28,000, Station Main, Edmonton AB T5J 4R4.

1. **Province of Alberta Alexander Rutherford Scholarships** are provided to approximately 6,000 graduating Alberta students who have achieved an average of 80 percent or better in grades 10, 11, and 12. Each student receives a $300 scholarship for a qualifying grade 10 average, $500 for a qualifying Grade 11 average and $700 for a qualifying grade 12 average. Application must be made by May 1 for September entry and December 1 for January entry to college or university.
2. **Rutherford Scholarships** are provided to the top 10 graduating students as determined on the basis of Diploma Examination results in English 30 or Français 30, Social Studies 30 and three other subjects. These students will become known as Rutherford Scholars and will receive a plaque and $1,500 in addition to their Alexander Rutherford Scholarship. Candidates will be selected from Alexander Rutherford Scholarship applications received prior to September 1.

3. **United World College Scholarships** are awarded to six grade 11 Alberta residents based on academic ability, leadership capability, references and an interview. This scholarship will provide for two years of study at United World Colleges. Application deadline is March 1. United World Colleges are located in Victoria, Canada; New Mexico, United States; Caracas, Venezuela; South Glamorgan, Wales, United Kingdom; Fjaler, Norway; Trieste, Italy; Mbabane, Swaziland; Bombay, India; Pasir, Singapore; and Hong Kong. The Canadian address is Lester B. Pearson College of the Pacific, R.R. 1, Victoria BC V9B 5T7.
4. **Adult High-School Equivalency Scholarships**, valued at $500, are awarded to 200 adults who have been out of school for three years, have achieved a minimum average of 80 percent as full-time students in courses required for entry into a post-secondary program and are nominated by their high school or community college. Nomination deadline is September 1.
5. **Citizenship Awards** are awarded to one graduating student from each high school in recognition of outstanding characteristics in academic ability, leadership in school-sponsored, community or extracurricular activities and a demonstrated willingness to place the good of others above personal ambitions. Nominations must be made by May 1.
6. **Louise McKinney Post-Secondary Scholarships** are awarded to 930 Alberta students to recognize and encourage continued academic achievement in undergraduate study. Scholarships are worth $1,500 at the undergraduate level and $3,500 at a professional level. Students at post-secondary colleges in Alberta should apply to the college awards office. Students studying outside Alberta need to apply to the Alberta Heritage Scholarship Fund. Application deadline is June 1.
7. **"Persons Case" Scholarships** ranging from $1,000–$5,000 are awarded to students whose studies will contribute to the advancement of women, or who are studying in non-traditional fields (engineering, science, etc.). Awards are based on program of studies, academic achievement and financial need. Application deadline is September 30.

8. **Charles S. Noble Scholarships for Study at Harvard** awards two scholarships of $10,000 to Alberta students for undergraduate study at Harvard. Prospective students should apply to the Alberta Heritage Scholarship Fund by May 15.
9. **Charles S. Noble Scholarships for Student Leadership** awards 80 scholarships, valued at $300 based on outstanding leadership in student government, student societies, clubs or organizations at the post-secondary level. Nomination deadline is March 1.
10. **Jimmie Condon Athletic Scholarships** provide approximately 1,400 scholarships valued at $1,000 each. These are awarded to students at post-secondary institutions in Alberta who are members of designated teams, maintaining an average of at least 65 percent and enrolled as full-time students. Nomination deadline is November 1.
11. **Charles S. Noble Junior Football Scholarships,** valued at $1,000, are awarded to 30 junior football players who are currently enrolled full-time in a post-secondary institution in Alberta and are nominated by their team. Nomination deadline is October 1.
12. **Charles S. Noble Junior A Hockey Scholarships,** valued at $650, are awarded to five individuals who are currently enrolled in full-time post-secondary study in Alberta and have participated in Junior A Hockey. Nominations must be submitted by the team by December 1.
13. **Michael Luchkovich Scholarships for Career Development** are offered to individuals who have demonstrated outstanding ability in their work and are pursuing short-term, full-time study of less than six months, or part-time study. Applicants must have worked in Alberta for a minimum of three years. Applications must be made by December 1, April 1 and August 1.
14. **Alberta Motion Picture Industry Training Program**

- On-the-job training awards of $200/week are provided to an employer to hire a trainee for up to six months. The trainee must be an Alberta resident being trained by a qualified craftsperson and cannot be replacing a qualified worker. Applications deadlines are January 15, May 15 and September 15.

- Short courses or seminar grants are available to individuals already established in the film or television industry to develop their skills. Application deadlines are January 15, May 15 and September 15.

15. **Northern Alberta Development Bursaries** are designed to increase the number of qualified professionals in Northern Alberta. Students who are committed to a life and career in the North are eligible to apply if they have been residents of Alberta for three years before applying. Awards are valued at $3,000. Recipients are required to live and work for one year within the Northern Alberta Development Council boundary upon graduation. Application deadline is May 31.
16. **Aboriginal Health Careers Bursaries** provide for approximately 20 bursaries for aboriginal students in Alberta entering their second or subsequent year of post-secondary training in a health field. Awards are valued at up to $12,000/year for college programs and $13,000/year for university programs.
17. **The Alberta Press Council Scholarship**, valued at $1,000, is awarded yearly to an Alberta high-school student enrolling in post-secondary studies. The award is based on the applicant's ability to write an essay on a specified topic. Application deadline is January 15.
18. **The Janet and Horace Allen Scholarship**, valued at $1,500, is awarded to the top science graduate from Crowsnest Pass High School who is an Alberta resident and has enrolled full-time in a post-secondary institution. Application deadline is June 1.
19. **The Theodore R. Campbell Scholarship**, valued at $1,500, is awarded to an aboriginal student studying Education at Blue Quills First Nation College. Applicants must be Alberta residents and in their second year of the Blue Quills University Transfer Program.
20. **CANA scholarships** were designed to recognize and reward the exceptional academic achievements of children of CANA employees. Applicants must be Alberta residents entering their second or subsequent year of study at an eligible institution.

One award of $1,500 and two awards of $1,000 are available each year. Application deadline is October 31.

21. **The Robert C. Carson Memorial Bursary** offers five awards of $500 to aboriginal Albertans without sponsorship enrolled full-time in their second year of the Law Enforcement, Criminal Justice Diploma or Faculty of Law programs at eligible institutions. Students who are seeking nominations for these awards should contact the financial aid office of their institution.
22. **The Hal Harrison Memorial Scholarship** awards one $250 scholarship to the grade 12 student with the highest marks who is enrolled full-time at a post-secondary institution and one of their parents is a member in good standing with the Alberta Volunteer Fire Fighters Association. Application deadline is June 1.
23. **The Anna & John Kolesar Memorial Scholarship**, valued at $1,200, is awarded to the applicant with the highest academic average in three designated subjects as shown on an Alberta Education Transcript. Applicants must be Alberta residents, planning to enroll in a faculty of education and from a family where neither parent has a university degree. Application deadline is July 1.
24. **Hal Neldner Scholarships and Telus Bursaries**, valued at $1,500 each, will be awarded to two top high-school graduates, two to the top post-secondary students and two random bursaries to students whose parents are employed by Telus and its wholly owned subsidiaries. Application deadline is June 1.
25. **Robin Rousseau Memorial Mountain Achievement Scholarship** was developed to recognize excellence in leadership development and safety in the mountain community. Applicants must be Alberta residents, active in the mountain community and must be planning on taking a recognized Mountain Leadership and Safety Certification Program. Value of the award varies and award will be made at the completion of the program. Application deadline is January 30.

26. **Staples Scholarships**, valued at $2,000 each, are awarded to the top two applicants entering the Faculty of Business or Commerce. Averages are calculated based on the final marks in five designated grade 12 courses. Application deadline is June 30.
27. **The Thygesen Scholarship**, valued at $500, is awarded to an apprenticeship student entering a second session of classroom study. Recipients are selected based on academic performance, financial need and employer recommendation. Application deadline is September 15.
28. **Summer Language Bursary Program** offers approximately 500 bursaries to provide an opportunity to learn French as a second language. Applicants must be Alberta residents and full-time students, enrolled or intending to enroll in post-secondary studies. Bursaries cover tuition and room and board for a five-week program. Application deadline is February 15.
29. **Decouverte** offers approximately 60 bursaries to provide an opportunity for francophones outside Quebec to improve their French-language skills. Applicants must be Alberta residents with French as a first language and full-time students in grades 11, 12 or post-secondary studies. Bursaries cover tuition, board and room, and a portion of the travel costs for the five-week program. Application deadline is February 15.
30. **Official-Language Monitor Program** (see Ontario program). Application deadline is February 15.
31. **Fellowships for Full-time Studies in French** are awarded to approximately 350 students to assist in pursuing post-secondary studies in French in any discipline in Canada. Applicants must be Alberta residents enrolled in a university. Awards are valued at $500–$1,000/semester, as well as $200 travel grant per semester for studies outside Alberta. Students enrolled in an education program may also qualify for the Roger Mahe Memorial Award. Application deadline is September 15.
32. **Fellowships for Full-time Studies in French** offers approximately 350 awards to assist francophone students pursuing studies in French at a college or technical institute in any discipline in Canada. Applicants must be Alberta residents with

French as a first language, enrolled full-time. Awards are valued at $1,000 per semester with a $200 travel grant for studies outside Alberta. Application deadline is September 15.

BRITISH COLUMBIA

1. **Premier's Excellence Awards** are bursaries, valued at $5,000 each, which are awarded to the top all-round graduating student in each of the 15 college regions in British Columbia.
2. **Financial Assistance for Native Indian Students** is availble to status Indians. Enquiries should be made to the appropriate band and further assistance may be available from any First Nations Centre.
3. **French Language Study Awards** are administered by Modern Languages & Multicultural Programs, Ministry of Education, c/o Parliament Buildings, Victoria BC V8V 1X4.
4. **Duke of Edinburgh Award** provides 10 bursaries of $500 each to residents of B.C. and Yukon who are in the program and have shown personal growth while meeting the challenges of the Duke of Edinburgh Award. Contact Duke of Edinburgh Award, 212-633 Courtney St., Victoria BC V8W 1B8.

MANITOBA

1. **French Language Assistance Programs** are available to students of Manitoba. For further information, contact:

   Provincial Co-ordinator
   Official Languages Programs
   Bureau de l'Education français
   Department of Education and Training
   509-1181 Portage Ave.
   Winnipeg MB R3G OT3

NEW BRUNSWICK

1. **Co-op Atlantic McEwen Scholarship** provides two scholarships, valued at $1,000 each, to applicants who are full-time employees or dependents of full-time employees of Co-op Atlantic or one of its member co-operatives. An essay of 500 words or more is required, relating past experiences, aspirations and the concept of co-operation. Contact: Manager, Corporate Administrative Services, Co-op Atlantic, P.O. Box 750, Moncton NB E1C 8N5.
2. **Donald E. Curren Scholarships** (see Nova Scotia listing).
3. **J. Harper Kent Charitable Foundation Scholarships** provide a varied number of awards based on academic achievement and financial need. Contact Montreal Trust Co., P.O. Box 100, Saint John NB E2L 3X7.
4. **The Modern Enterprises LTD Scholarship,** valued at $2,500 over four to five years, is available to a student studying for a BSc in Engineering. The award is based on academics and extracurricular activity. Contact Awards Committee, Modern Enterprises, Moncton NB E2L 3X7.
5. **Purdy MacDonald Scholarship** offers several awards of $500. Contact Purdy MacDonald Charitable Foundation, c/o TD Bank and Trust, P.O. Box 756, Fredericton NB E3B 5B6.
6. **French Language Awards** are available from the Department of Education and Labour at P.O. Box 6000, 548 York St., Fredericton NB E3B 5H1.
   Internet: www.gov.nb.ca/ael/strasse.htm
7. **Thelma Sewell Memorial Scholarship** offers $1,295 to a New Brunswick high-school graduate who demonstrates a genuine interest in home economics or a related area. Application deadline is May 31. Application forms are available from the New Brunswick Department of Education.
8. **Wendy's Classic Achiever High School Scholarship Awards** Program offers two scholarships of $6,000 each to a male and female student, and 10 other $1,000 scholarships to students from the Maritimes. Students must be nominated by their high schools. Students are nominated on the basis of academic standing in conjunction with school and/or community involvement.

Minimum average is 70 percent. Contact your school guidance counsellor or Wendy's Classic Achiever Scholarship Awards, P.O. Box 585, Department W, Pickering ON L1V 3T3.

NEWFOUNDLAND

1. **Centenary of Responsible Government Scholarships** provides 55 awards, valued at $1,000 each, to high-school grads who attain the highest marks in the scholarship exam, provided they have not already been awarded another government scholarship. See your high-school principal or guidance counsellor.
2. **Constable W. C. Moss Scholarship** offers $1,000 to the son or daughter of a member of the Royal Newfoundland Constabulary or the RCMP who has been a resident of the province for 12 months or a retired or deceased member of either of these forces. The award is based on the scholarship exam. See your high-school principal or guidance counsellor.
3. **Electoral District Scholarships**, valued at $1,000 each, are available to high-school graduates who attain the highest marks on the scholarship exam in the electoral districts where the students reside. See your high-school principal or guidance counsellor.
4. **Junior Jubilee Scholarship,** valued at $2,500, is offered to the high-school graduate who attains the highest marks in the scholarship exam. See your high-school principal or guidance counsellor.
5. **French Language Programs.** Additional information is available from: Division of Program Development, Language Programs Section, Department of Education, P.O. Box 8700, St. John's NF A1B 4J6.
6. **Co-op Atlantic McEwen Scholarship** (see New Brunswick listing).
7. **Wendy's Classic Achiever High School Scholarship Awards** Program (see New Brunswick listing).

NORTHWEST TERRITORIES

1. **Grade 12 Scholarships**, valued at $500, are awarded to Northwest Territory residents who achieve an average of 80 percent or more in grade 12 in a Northwest Territories school. These students must be enrolling in a post-secondary school and have made a formal request for this scholarship to the Student Financial Assistance Program.
2. **Undergraduate Scholarships**, valued at $750, are provided to students who achieve an A average in the first, second or third years of post-secondary studies. Students must be enrolled in a full course load. Make a request for this scholarship to the Student Financial Assistance Program.
3. **Native Graduate Scholarships**, valued at $1,500, are provided to students eligible for supplementary grants for any year of a master's or doctoral program in which the student achieves a B average. The student must take a full course load and make a request in writing to the Student Financial Assistance Program. Recipients of this undergraduate scholarship are not eligible for the Master's and Doctorate Scholarships.

NOVA SCOTIA

1. **French Language Bursaries** are available in Nova Scotia by obtaining application forms from French Language Bursaries, Department of Education, P.O. Box 578, Trade Mart Building, Halifax NS B3J 2S9.
2. **Co-op Atlantic McEwen Scholarships** (see New Brunswick listing).
3. **Donald E. Curran Scholarships** provide four $1,000 and four $500 awards to mobility-impaired students with preference for paraplegic and quadriplegic students. These scholarships are based on academic standing. Contact Donald E. Curran Scholarship Fund, Canadian Paraplegic Association, 1310 Hollis St., Ste. 150, Halifax NS B3J 3P3.
4. **Wendy's Classic Achiever High School Scholarship Awards** Program (see New Brunswick listing).

ONTARIO

Many scholarships, bursaries and loans for Ontario students are awarded through OSAP, the Ontario Student Assistance Program. Applications are available at high school guidance offices and by writing directly to Student Support Branch, Ministry of Education and Training, P.O. Box 4500, Thunder Bay ON P7B 6G7.
OSAP administers a number of programs:

- Bursary for Students with Disabilities
- Child Care Bursary Plan
- Ontario Special Bursary Plan
- Ontario Work-study Plan

Other post-secondary programs are administered by the Student Support Branch of the Ministry of Education and Training. These include:

- Aird Scholarship
- Fellowships for Studying in French
- Ontario Graduate Scholarships
- Ontario-Quebec Exchange Fellowship
- Summer Language Bursary Program

1. **The Aird Scholarship** offers two scholarships of $2,500 to help student with physical disabilities to study in the first year of a full-time program at a recognized Ontario post-secondary institution. Students are required to demonstrate outstanding achievement, motivation and initiative.
2. **Ontario Housing Corporation Bursary Program** is available to students who are tenants of Ontario's public housing system. The bursaries provide $500 for each of two years. As well, there are awarts for tenants enrolling in short-term academic or skills trading. Contact Ontario Housing Corporation, Southern Regional Office, 119 King Street West, 14th Floor, Hamilton ON L8P 4Y7.
3. **OTIP/RAEO** offers four bursaries of $2,500 each to children or dependents of OTIP/RAEO clients. Contact OTIP/RAEO Academic Bursary Program, c/o Department of Human Resources, 125 Northfield Drive West, P.O. Box 218, Waterloo ON N2J 3Z9.

4. **Wendy's Classic Achiever High School Scholarship Awards Program** offers two scholarships, of $6,000 each, to a male and female student and ten other $1,000 scholarship to students from Ontario (see New Brunswick listing).

Check your college/university calendar

Many scholarships. bursaries and prizes in Ontario - and elsewhere - are awarded by the university or college to which you are applying. At McMaster University, for instance, over 65 individual scholarships are listed in the calendar and on their website. These are listed alphabetically from The Association of Professional Engineers Scholarship to the Zonta Club of Hamilton - Roberta Bondar - McMaster Scholarships. Ordinarily your general application for financial aid will constitute an application to those scholarships that are available in your discipline, but it pays to check the fine print for every scholarship available at the school you want to attend.

PRINCE EDWARD ISLAND

1. **Canadian Legion National Scholarships** are awarded to children or descendents of veterans. For application forms contact: Secretary of Royal Canadian Legion, P.E.I. Command, P.O. Box 134, Charlottetown PE C1A 7K2.
2. **Donald E. Curran Scholarships** (see Nova Scotia listing).
3. **Co-op Atlantic McEwen Scholarships** (see New Brunswick listing).
4. **Wendy's Classic Achiever High School Scholarship Awards Program** (see New Brunswick listing).

QUEBEC

For additional information on any of the scholarships listed below contact Student Financial Aid, Loans and Bursary Services, Complex G, 22nd Floor, Quebec PQ G1R 5A5.

1. **The Canadian-Chinese Cultural Society of Montreal Inc. Scholarship** is available to a Montreal student who is interested in Chinese culture. The scholarship is based on academic achievement and participation in extracurricular activites. Applications are due on February 28.
2. **Engineers Association Student Trust Fund** provides scholarships and bursaries to students of Hungarian origin or descent. These awards are based on scholastic achievement, career plans, character and financial need.
3. **La Foundation Girardin-Vaillancourt** offers an award to a Canadian citizen who is a Quebec resident and studying one of the following disciplines: co-operatives, economics, finance, administration, science or arts. Applications are due on March 1.
4. **Lebanese-Syrian-Canadian Association Scholarships** are provided to students of Lebanese-Syrian origin.
5. **St. Laurent Cement Inc.** offers an award to students who are dependents of current or retired employees, or of an employee who died while employed by the company. Application deadline is June 25.
6. **Quebec Federation of the Blind Inc. Bursary** is available from Activities Co-ordinator, Quebec Federation of the Blind Inc., Room 115, 7000 Sherbrooke St. W., Montreal PQ H4B 1R3.

SASKATCHEWAN

1. **Saskatchewan Awards Program** provides 650 general proficiency awards to the top academic students in Saskatchewan secondary schools. Each award is valued at $400. Students must be nominated by their schools.
2. **Donald R. Simmons Memorial Scholarships** are awarded annually to two Saskatchewan students of First Nations or Métis ancestry who are enrolled in an approved post-secondary school and who will not be a recipient of a general proficiency award. Students must apply to Saskatchewan Post-Secondary Education and Skills Training, 3085 Albert St., Regina SK S4P 3V7.

YUKON

1. **Yukon Excellence Awards** are awarded to students of the Yukon based on their academic performance at the secondary school level. Any student who writes Yukon Territorial Examinations and B.C. Provincial Examinations is eligible. To qualify for an award students must attain a mark of 80 percent or better. Application for the award can be made anytime during the school year, but must be redeemed within 10 years after leaving high school. Application is made on the Student Financial Assistance Application. No amount is stipulated.
2. **Duke of Edinburgh Award** provides 10 $500 awards to students of the Yukon who actively participate in the Duke of Edinburgh Award program, an international program for all young people between the ages of 14 and 25 years. Participants earn awards by completing requirements in community service, skills, physical fitness and expeditions. Contact: The Duke of Edinburgh Award, British Columbia & Yukon Divison, 212-633 Courtney St., Victoria BC V8W 1B8.

FEDERAL-PROVINCIAL PROGRAMS

Application to these programs can be made at secondary-school guidance offices, university or college French departments or the Ministry of Education and Training, Official Languages Monitor Program, Mowat Block, 900 Bay St., 16th Floor, Toronto ON M7A 1L2.

1. **Summer Language Bursary Program** awards bursaries to students to undertake a summer immersion course in their second official language, either French or English. Bursary covers tuition and board and room.
2. **Bursary Program for Francophones Outside Quebec** provides bursaries for eligible francophone students whose first language is French and who reside in Ontario to take a summer course in French at specific locations in Quebec and New Brunswick. Bursary covers tuition and board and room.
3. **Fellowships for Studying in French** are provided to approximately 800 students based on academic merit to enter full-time post-secondary studies in which the language of instruction

is French. Students must be enrolling for the first time in an eligible French-language or bilingual university in Canada, a bilingual or French-language college of applied arts and technology in Ontario, a bilingual or French-language approved post-secondary institution in Canada or a professional program in a French-language CEGEP in Quebec. A supplement of $1,000 may be available if the program is not offered within 80 km of the applicant's permanent residence.

4. **The Official-Languages Monitor Program** is designed for French-speaking or English-speaking students to help them improve their second-language skills while teaching their first language. As monitors, students act as resource persons and assist teachers in educational activities.

- Full-Time Monitor Program provides students with a work period from September to May and renumeration of $11,400. These students must have completed at least one year of university study or of their diplome d'études collegiales in Quebec and are prepared to assume the duties of a monitor. Monitors are normally required to leave their home province and be assigned to a rural or semi-rural area.
- Part-time Monitor Program provides renumeration of $3,500 for full-time university students in Canada who, by June 1996, have completed at least one year of university study or their diplome d'études collegiales in Quebec and who are prepared to work part-time as second language monitors in educational institutions. This program generally applies to monitors who are working and studying outside their home province.

It is important to realize that the above list constitutes only the federally and provincially administered scholarships. There are many scholarships offered by corporate and private donors in each province that were not listed here. Some are in the next chapter.

CHAPTER SEVEN

Private foundations and corporations

There is a wealth of scholarships that are offered Canada-wide by private organizations. The effort that is needed to acquaint yourself with them can be well worth your while if even one or two pay off for you.

Upon completing your list of scholarships that you are eligible for and wish to apply for, you would be well advised to approach your school guidance counsellor with that list to seek copies of any application forms that the school has on hand. You will need to write for those forms that are not catalogued in your school.

1. **A.A. Heaps.** Two scholarships of $3,000 are offered annually to students based on a 1,000-word essay on the contributions made by A.A. Heaps to social reform in Canadian life. Deadline May 15. Contact your school guidance counsellor or A.A. Heaps Scholarship Committee, Canadian Labour Congress, Educational Services, 301-2841 Riverside Dr., Ottawa ON K1V 8X7.
2. **AGF Scholarships.** Forty scholarships valued at $2,080 - $1,000 for tuition and $1,080 invested on your behalf over three years - are granted throughout Canada. A minimum average of 75 percent is required. Application deadline is May 29. See your guidance counsellor for more information or contact AGF Financial Life Skills Scholarship, York/Toronto 1833, 260 Adelaide St. E., P.O. Box 51, Toronto ON M5A 1N1.
3. **Allard Broadcast Journalism Scholarship.** An award valued at $2,000 is available to a student who is enrolled in a broadcast journalism program. The student must exhibit strong leadership qualities, as well as the desire to assist others in the industry.

Applicants are requested to write a 500-word essay explaining their career goals, why they are interested in broadcast journalism and how the scholarship will help to reach those goals. Application deadline is June 30. Contact: The Canadian Association of Broadcasters, P.O. Box 627, Station B, Ottawa ON K1P 5S2.

4. **John Brooks Community Foundation.** These awards are based on academic achievement and outstanding ability in such areas as community service, arts or sciences. For further information, contact John Brooks Community Foundation, 21 Vaughan Rd. Ste. 203B, Toronto ON M6G 2N2.
5. **Canadian Association of Principals Senior Student Leadership Award.** In 1997-98, 21 recipients received scholarships of $500. Schools are asked to nominate one student leader who has demonstrated outstanding leadership and has achieved in the top 20 percent of the class. Application forms are available at the school. Each secondary school is eligible to sponsor a nominee for the C.A.P. Student Leadership Award. Students are requested to complete a questionnaire. Nomination and questionaire must be postmarked by March 31. See your school guidance counsellor for more information.
6. **1989 Canadian Engineering Memorial Foundation Scholarship Awards.** This award valued at $5,000 is available to a female student entering engineering who has demonstrated outstanding academic achievement and community leadership. For more information contact: 1989 Canadian Engineering Memorial Scholarships, Ste. 401, 116 Albert St., Ottawa ON K1P 5G3.
7. **Canadian Hospitality Foundation.** The Canadian Hospitality Foundation offers seven annual university entrance scholarships ranging from $1,000 to $2,000. The applicants must be in their final year of secondary school and must enter a hospitality degree program at the University of Guelph, Mount Saint Vincent University, University of Calgary or Ryerson Polytechnic University.
8. **Canadian Library Association.** Several scholarships valued at $1,000-$2,500 are awarded annually to students entering an accredited library school in North America. Applications and additional information can be obtained from: Canadian Library Association, 200 Elgin St., Ste. 602, Ottawa ON K2P 1L5.

9. **Canadian Merit Scholarship Foundation.** This is a collection of scholarships for students who have a strong list of community involvement, leadership activities, extracurricular activities and academics. Scholarships range from $500 to $26,000. In 1997-98, 3,012 students applied for 159 money awards and 29 honor citations. Total value of awards is over $1.5 million in 1999. See your school guidance counsellor for application forms. It is an advantage to be school-sponsored. Students may choose to be school-sponsored or apply directly. Deadline for sponsored applications is October 27, for direct applications November 18.
10. **Canadian Printing Industries Scholarship Trust Fund Scholarship.** Canadian Printing Industries Association provides financial assistance to deserving students requiring educational assistance. To be eligible the student must be interested in a career in some aspect of the printing and allied industries (management, design, technology, etc.) and have a good academic record. Awards vary from $100 to 600/year up to a maximum of four years. Contact: Canadian Printing Industries Scholarship Trust Fund, 75 Albert St., Fuller Building, Ste. 906, Ottawa Canada K1P 5E7.
11. **Canadian Seed Growers' Association Bursary.** A bursary of $300 is to be awarded to a rural student in the first, second or third year of a Bachelor of Science in Agriculture at the College of Agriculture. The award will be given on the basis of both scholarship and need, and preference will be given to students entering the first year. Application forms may be obtained from the Dean of Agriculture, University of Saskatchewan, Saskatoon SK S7N OWO.
12. **Canadian Society of Exploration Geophysicists, Calgary.** Several awards of up to $1,500 are available to students majoring in geophysics based on academic standing and financial need. Contact: Canadian Society of Exploration Geophysicists Scholarship Trust Fund, 406, 206-7 Ave. SW, Calgary AB T2P 0W7.
13. **CanWest Global System Broadcasters of the Future Awards.** This award, valued at up to $4,000, is available to a

student who is a member of a self-identified visible minority and entering a radio and television arts program or journalism. Application deadline is May 31. Contact: CanWest Global System - BFA, 81 Barber Greene Rd., Don Mills ON M3C 2A2.

14. **CN Scholarship Program for Women.** Fifty-five scholarships, valued at $500 each, are available to women who are studying to enter non-traditional fields related to the transportation industry. Contact: Employment Equity, Canadian National, 935 rue de la Gauchetière O., 7th Floor, Montreal PQ H3B 2M9.
15. **CSEA/Berol Prismacolor National Art Scholarships.** Three awards, valued at $1,000 each, are available to students entering fine arts, based on outstanding visual artistic ability. A portfolio must be submitted with the application. Deadline is May 29. Contact: CSEA-Berol Commission Scolaire Les Ecores, 647 Lesage, Laval PQ H7E 2Y6.
16. **Canada Trust Scholarships for Outstanding Community Leadership.** This scholarship was launched in 1995. Students are rewarded for outstanding community leadership in balance with personal circumstances and academic performance. Each scholarship includes full tuition for up to four years of undergraduate study at a college or university in Canada, plus $3,500 a year towards living expenses for up to four years as well as a guaranteed offer of summer employment at Canada Trust during the years of the scholarship. Twenty such scholarships are awarded each year. There are also 60 runner-up awards of $500. Applications are available at all high schools and Canada Trust branches or see your school guidance counsellor. If you have questions, check the Internet at www. canadatrust. com.
17. **Canadian Water Resources Association.** Three scholarships of $1,250 are awarded for graduate students whose programs of study focus on applied, natural or social science aspects of water resources. See your school guidance counsellor for application forms.
18. **Charolais Youth Scholarship.** This scholarship, valued at $400, is awarded to students involved in agriculture, who are studying in a field that will enhance agriculture. Applications

must be received by October 1. Contact your school guidance counsellor for application forms or Canadian Charolais Association, 2320-41 Ave. NE, Calgary AB T2E 6W8.

19. **Dental and Paramedical Bursaries.** These bursaries are available to students enrolled in a college of dentistry or in a paramedical course leading to a public health specialty, such as clinical or educational psychology, dental health, social work, physiotherapy, occupational therapy, psychiatric nursing, psychiatry, public health inspector, speech therapist, respiratory therapist, and nuclear medicine technologist. For further information and applications contact: Director of Professional Training, Department of Public Health, 3211 Albert St., Regina SK S4S 5W6.

20. **Fel-Pro Automotive Technicians Scholarship Program.** High-school seniors, graduates, GED or post-secondary students who are enrolled or planning to enroll in a full-time course of study in automotive technology at any accredited post-secondary institution in the United States or Canada are eligible to apply for this scholarship. Scholarship is valued at $500 (U.S.)/year of study. See your school guidance counsellor for application forms. Deadline is May 1.

21. **Food Service and Hospitality Scholarships.** Two scholarships of $2,000/year are awarded to persons with physical disabilities who are accepted as full-time students into a post-secondary degree or diploma program in food service or hospitality at a university or college in Canada. Scholarships are awarded on scholastic achievement. One scholarship each year is awarded to Region A (Quebec and Eastern Canada) and one in Region B (Ontario and Western Canada). See your school guidance counsellor for application forms or contact: Canadian Food Service Executive Association, 1531 Bayview Ave., Ste. 3529, Toronto ON M4G 4G8.

22. **La Foundation Donation Frement.** Awards of varying value are available to students planning to study in French. Contact: La Foundation Donation Frement Inc., 325 rue Dalhousie, pièce 702, Ottawa ON K1N 7G2.

23. **Girl Guides of Canada.** Girl Guides award two scholarships annually to students across Canada, who are studying in certain fields and continuing their involvement with Guides. Applications may be obtained from Roberta Bondar, Scholarship Administrator, Girl Guides of Canada, 50 Merton St., Toronto ON M4S 1A3.
24. **Elizabeth Greenshields Foundation.** Grants valued up to $10,000 are available to students who are planning to study arts with the purpose of making it a career. Contact: Elizabeth Greenshields Foundation, 1814 Sherbrooke St. W., Montreal PQ H3H 1E4.
25. **John Gyles Education Fund.** Scholarships valued up to $3,000 are available based on academic achievement, financial need and other criteria. Contact: John Gyles Education Fund, P.O. Box 4808, Station A, Fredericton NB E3B 5G4.
26. **Ruth Hancock Scholarships.** Three scholarships, valued at $2,000 each, are awarded to students who are entering a recognized communications course and planning to enter a career in Canadian broadcasting. Applicants are required to demonstrate strong leadership qualities. Applications include a 500-word essay stating career goals and how the scholarship will help the student to attain those goals. Application deadline is June 30. Contact: The Canadian Association of Broadcasters, P.O. Box 627, Station B, Ottawa ON K1P 5A2.
27. **Hal Rogers Endowment Fund.** This fund was established in 1996 to honor the legacy of the founder of Kinsmen and Kinettes, Harold Allin Rogers (1899–1994). This award, valued at $1,000, is open to students across Canada who demonstrate superior academic performance, as well as community and extracurricular involvement. In 1997, 33 awards were given. For more information and application forms contact: Kinsmen & Kinette Clubs of Canada, 1920 Hal Rogers Dr., P.O. Box KIN, Cambridge ON N3H 5C6.
28. **Ivomec Trust Fund 4-H Scholarship.** There were 50 to 100 Ivomec scholarships, of $1,000 each, established across Canada in 1998. These scholarships are available to 4-H members to further their agriculture-related studies at a university or col-

lege. Application deadline is March 31. Scholarship information is available at 4-H offices.

29. **Jack Moore Memorial Scholarships.** Twelve scholarships of $300 each, in addition to 12 bursaries of $300 each, are offered to students who are attending their first year at university, technical school or business college in 1998. The scholarships are based on academic standing. The bursaries are based on academic standing and financial need. They are available to direct descendants of veterans, ex-service and current military members and RCMP personnel. Application must be received by August 28. See your school guidance counsellor for application forms.
30. **Knights of Columbus Pro Deo and Pro Patria (Canada) Scholarships.** Eligible candidates are members or sons or daughters of members of the Canadian Council of the Knights of Columbus who are entering the first year of a Canadian university degree program.The maximum scholarship is valued at $1,500. Deadline is May 1. For application forms and more information contact: Director of Scholarship Aid, Knights of Columbus, P.O. Box 1670, New Haven CT 06507-0901.
31. **Lindsey Morden Claim Services Ltd.** This scholarship is intended for relatives of an individual employed in the insurance industry. It is also intended for students who intend to train for employment in that industry. One $1,000 scholarship is awarded in each province and territory in Canada. The application must be received by July 31 in each province and territory except for Newfoundland where the deadline is August 31. Contact: Lindsey Morden Claim Services Limited, 155 University Ave., Ste. 600, Toronto ON M5H 3N5.
32. **Magna for Canada Scholarships.** Ten awards of $5,000 and one national award of $10,000 are available. Students must submit an essay on the topic "If you were Prime Minister of Canada, what would you do to improve living standards and unify the country?" Application deadline is June 15. Contact: Magna for Canada Scholarship, 337 Magna Dr., Aurora ON L4G 7K1.
33. **Mathieu Da Costa Awards Program.** Elementary and secondary-school students in Canada are eligible to enter. Students

from ages 9-13 are required to write an essay of 500 words; 14-19-year-old students are required to write 1000-word essays. Submissions should demonstrate an effort to explore and widen the horizons of Canada's rich history and help the reader to appreciate the enormous contributions made by people of diverse origins in building our nation. Students are encouraged to research and present stories of people about whom published material is available, as well as others whose contributions are not so well documented. There are also categories for best artistic representation for ages 9-13, 14-16 and 17-19. Six prizes of $300 will be awarded. Entry deadline is December 11. For more information check the Internet: www.ctf-fce.ca

34. **Mensa Canada Scholarships.** Applicants are required to write a 500-word essay describing specific goals (academic, vocational or career) that the scholarship will help achieve. Applicants must be in full-time attendance at an accredited post-secondary institution. Deadline is February 28. See your school guidance counsellor for application forms or contact: Mensa Canada Scholarship Program, 329 March Rd. Ste. 232, P.O. Box 11, Kanata ON K2K 2E1.
35. **Miller Thomson Foundation.** These awards are available based on academic abilities and contribution to school and community. Application deadline is March 31. Contact: Executive Director, Miller Thompson Foundation, 20 Queen St. W., Ste. 2500, Toronto ON M5H 3S1.
36. **Monsanto Agribusiness Scholarship**. This scholarship is for high-school students from family farms who are enrolled at a Canadian educational institution in first-year agriculture, agri-science or management. Ten high-school students each from Alberta, Saskatchewan, Manitoba, Ontario, and Quebec will be awarded scholarships of $1,000 each. Application deadline is August 15. See the school guidance counsellor or 4-H offices for application forms.
37. **Orville Erickson Memorial Scholarship**. These scholarships, which are awarded in June and December, are for students in need of financial assistance pursuing a career related to conservation and the environment. Applications may be sub-

mitted anytime during the year. Students will be notified by February 1 and August 1. Applications are available from: Orville Erickson Memorial Scholarship Fund, Canadian Wildlife Foundation, 2740 Queensview Dr., Ottawa ON K2B 1A2.

38. **Padgett Business Services Scholarship Program.** One international award of $4,000 and several local $500 awards are available to dependents of small business owners. The business must have less than 20 employees. The owners must own at least 10 percent of the stock or capital in the business and be active in the day-to-day operation of the business. Applications include transcripts, test scores, an essay and information about the family business. Application is due on March 1. Contact your local Padgett Business Services.

39. **Petro-Canada Back-to-school Bursary Program.** These bursaries, worth $400, $500 and $800, are offered to Petro-Canada employees who have been a guest service attendant/employee for at least six months. Applicants are required to complete an application form and write an essay on a predetermined topic. See your Petro-Canada employer for application forms. Deadline is February 28.

40. **Reader's Digest Valedictorian Award.** Reader's Digest offers one-year subscriptions as awards to the valedictorians of all graduating classes of Canadian high schools. Each recipient also receives a gift certificate. Interested school principals are asked to forward the names and home addresses of valedictorians (as many as two per school), typewritten on school letterhead to: Valedictorian Subscription Program, Reader's Digest Magazines Ltd., 215 Redern Ave., Westmount PQ H3Z 2V9.

41. **Sask Power and Youth Interculture Canada Scholarship.** This scholarship is offered to students aged 15-17 who would like to live and study in a foreign country for a year. An essay of 1,500-2,000 words is part of the application. See your guidance counsellor for application forms.

42. **Society of Graphic Designers of Canada (Cam Jansen Scholarship Award).** A scholarship of $500 is awarded to a student who has chosen graphic design as a career and who applies with a portfolio of designs and an essay. See the school

guidance counsellor for an application form or write to: Cam Jansen Scholarship, c/o NEXT Communications Inc., 201-302 Pacific Ave., Saskatoon SK S7K 1P1. Applications must be received by May 31.

43. **Soil and Water Conservation Society Environmental Sciences Scholarship.** Eligible students need to have a cumulative high school average of at least 75 percent and be accepted to a post-secondary program in agriculture, geography, engineering or a related discipline with a natural resource conservation-related curriculum, as well as demonstrate involvement in conservation or environmental activities during high school. See the school guidance counsellor for application forms. Applications must be received by May 1.
44. **St. John Ambulance Bursaries.** Bursaries are available to persons trained by St. John Ambulance who wish to continue their studies in a paramedical/medical field. Applications must be received by March 15. Contact: St. John Ambulance Association, 312 Laurier Ave. E., Ottawa ON K1N 6P6.
45. **Soroptimist Training Awards Program.** This program aids mature women who must enter or return to the job market. Candidates should be heads of households completing undergraduate programs or entering vocational or technical training programs. Applications must be received by December 15. Contact: TAP Awards Committee, Box 8937, Saskatoon SK S7K 6S7.
46. **Soroptimist Youth Citizenship Awards.** These awards recognize young people for their outstanding contributions to home, school, community, country and the world. They are *not* awarded for scholastic achievement, but for the applicant's demonstrated commitment to improving the quality of life for others. Contact the address above.
47. **Tandy Leather Company.** Four scholarships of $1,000, $750, $500 and $250 are offered to senior high-school students who create a scholarship entry made of at least 50 percent leather and have definite plans to continue their education. The entry must be accompanied by a 250-word summary of experience and an application form. See the school guidance counsellor

for application forms or contact: Tandy Leather Co., P.O. Box 13,000, 120 Brock St., Barrie ON L4M 4W4. Application must be received by April 1.

48. **Terry Fox Humanitarian Scholarships.** These scholarships, valued at $4,000 annually for up to four years, are renewable and available to students enrolling in post-secondary education who have demonstrated high ideals, citizenship, humanitarian service and high achievement in academic, sport and health endeavors. One of the main criteria is "overcoming obstacles." Information and forms available from: Terry Fox Humanitarian Award Program, 711-151 Sparks St., Ottawa ON K1P 5E3. Deadline February 1.

49. **The Leonard Foundation Scholarships.** These scholarships were established to assist those students who would be unable to get an education without financial assistance. Preference is given to children of clergy, school teachers, military personnel, graduates of the Royal Military Colleges of Canada and members of the Mining and Metallurgical Institutes of Canada. Full-time students who are enrolled in an undergraduate college or university may apply. If the gross annual income of the family exceeds $40,000, the student is not likely to receive a scholarship. This scholarship averages $1,250 and approximately 140 are given each year across Canada. Students are advised to begin the application process as soon as first term results are available to complete the process by March 15. Each applicant must contact a nominator to arrange an interview before the application deadline. See your guidance counsellor for application forms or contact The Leonard Foundation, 20 Eglinton Ave. W. 7th Floor, Toronto ON M4R 2E2.

50. **UGG Members' Scholarship.** Ten scholarships of $600/year for four years are awarded to two students who are dependents of United Grain Growers' members of Alberta-British Columbia, Saskatchewan, Manitoba, and the balance of the four selected randomly across the provinces. See your guidance counsellor for an application or a United Grain Growers' agent. Applications must be received by July 1.

51. **University of Toronto National Book Awards.** Each school is invited to choose one outstanding academic student from the graduating year. The school will receive a National Book Award to present to that student on behalf of the University of Toronto. The candidate must be a Canadian citizen. Application forms are sent to each high school in fall or forms may be requested from: Admissions and Awards, University of Toronto, 315 Bloor St., W., Toronto ON M5S 1A3. Deadline is December 6.
52. **Western Conference of Teamsters Scholarship**. These scholarships are available to children of members of the Teamsters Union. Apply before February 15 to: Easter Conference of Teamsters Scholarship Committee, 1870 Ogden Dr., Burlingame CA 94010.
53. **Youth Merit Awards.** These awards recognize the outstanding accomplishments and contributions made to society by young Canadians in a variety of areas. Nominees must be 19 years or younger. See the guidance counsellor for an application form. Deadline for nominations is June 30.

CHAPTER EIGHT

Armed forces awards/scholarships

The high professional ability required of present-day military officers demands the best in education and training. The Department of National Defence therefore sponsors programs of university education and leadership training for selected young men and women who have the potential to become officers in the Canadian Armed Forces. The admission standards are high, but for those who qualify the way is open to a challenging and rewarding career. The programs sponsored are the Regular Officers Training Plan (ROTP), Medical Officers Training Plan (MOTP), Dental Officers Training Plan (DOTP) and Reserve Entry Training Plan (RETP). Training given under these plans is divided into two parts: normal attendance at university throughout the academic year and military training each summer.

ROTP. This plan combines university subsidization with career training as an officer in the regular component of the Canadian Armed Forces. Successful applicants are enrolled at the Royal Military Academy or a civilian university with the rank of officer cadet. They are required to maintain a good standing both academically and militarily while in the plan. All tuition, books, instruments and supplies are paid for by the Department of National Defence. In addition, the officer cadet receives a monthly salary. Free medical and dental care is provided. Annual leave (20 working days) with full pay and allowances may be granted each year, usually after the summer training period. On graduation the officer cadet is promoted to the commissioned rank of second lieutenant and serves for a specified time, usually in the armed forces. The normal period of obligatory service is five years, but this may be reduced to three years if the candidate attended a civilian university and required less than a full period of academic subsidization.

MOTP. Sponsorship is provided under the Medical Officer Training Plan during the third, fourth and fifth medicine and internship year. The program offers paid tuition, books and instruments, complete medical and dental coverage, paid holidays and monthly pay. Upon obtaining your license to practice medicine, you are promoted to the rank of captain and required to serve in the Canadian Armed Forces for three to five years.

DOTP. Sponsorship is provided under the Dental Officer Training Plan during the second, third, fourth and fifth year dentistry. Subsidization consists of paid tuition, books and instruments, complete medical and dental coverage, paid holidays and monthly pay. Upon receiving your license to practice dentistry, you are promoted to the rank of captain and required to serve a period of three to five years obligatory service in the Canadian Armed Forces.

RETP. This plan provides a limited number of vacancies for those students who would like to undertake military training along with their education, but who do not wish to commit themselves to regular force service after graduation. Reserve-entry cadets receive the same training and education as do ROTP cadets, but they are required to pay fees. These cadets do receive pay and allowances for the summer cadet training that they must take. Part-time service in the Primary Reserve for five years following graduation is encouraged.

Admission Requirements

An applicant must:

- be a Canadian citizen
- be physically fit
- if ROTP, be at least 16 years of age on the first of January the year commencing studies at university

Interested students are requested to contact:

Commanding Officer
Canadian Forces Recruiting Centre
101-22nd St. E., Room 413
Saskatoon SK S7K 0E1
or
Canadian Armed Forces Recruiting
Centre Regina
1820 Hamilton St., Room 110
Regina SK S4P 4K7

For further information or recruiting contact:
Registrar
Royal Military College of Canada
P.O. Box 17000, Station Forces
Kingston ON K7K 5L0
E-mail: registrar@rmc.ca
Internet: www.dnd.ca
or www.rmc.ca

BURSARIES AND SCHOLARSHIPS FOR MILITARY PERSONNEL

1. **Canadian Army Welfare Fund Bursaries.** All applicants must be dependent children of serving, retired or deceased members who served in the Canadian army (regular) between October 1, 1946, and January 31, 1968. Bursaries will be awarded particularly on the basis of financial need and are applicable at any Canadian university or technical institute. Application forms may be obtained from: The Manager, Canadian Army Welfare Foundation, Veteran Affairs Building, Lyon and Wellington St., Ottawa ON K1A 9P4.
2. **Royal Canadian Naval Benevolent Fund.** Financial assistance in the form of grants and loans are available to dependents of former members of the Naval Forces of Canada. Make application to the nearest Naval Division or District Office of the Department of Veterans' Affairs, P.O. Box 505, Station B, Ottawa ON K1P 5P6.

3. **Royal United Services Bursary.** This bursary of $400 is available to a student entering first-year studies, with preference to an applicant taking agriculture or related studies. The winning applicant must have a minimum grade 12 average of 75 percent, and be the son or daughter or ward of a member of United Services and Primary Reserves or a member of Army Cadets. Deadline August 10. Contact Manager of Royal United Services Institute, 1660 Elphinstone St., Regina SK S4T 3N1.
4. **Royal Canadian Air Force Benevolent Fund.** This fund provides assistance with post-secondary education in the form of an interest-free loan up to $2,000 per student or $4,000 per family. This assistance is based on eligibility and financial need. Contact: Royal Canadian Air Force Benevolent Fund, Ste. 302, Legion House, 359 Kent St., Ottawa ON K2P 0R6.
5. **Strathcona Trust Fund Scholarships.** An award of $750 is provided for two students who have completed grade 12 in the past year, were enrolled as members of a cadet corps/squadron for a minimum of two years, and are enrolled in a Canadian university with a major in physical education, education or recreation management. For further information and application forms, see your guidance counsellor or contact Lord Strathcona Trust Fund, Alberta Provincial Committee, Cadet Detachment Edmonton, Canadian Forces Base Edmonton, P.O. Box 10,500, Edmonton AB T5J 4J5 or Prairie Region, Cadet Detachment Regina, The Queen Building, 2800 Broad St., Regina SK S4P 4K6, ATTN: Secretary Lord Strathcona Trust Fund.

CHAPTER NINE

Athletic awards

Most students have heard of the substantial scholarships, awards and incentives given by American schools to top athletes in sports such as football, basketball and hockey. If you're in that league, the recruiters will come to you - this book won't make it happen.

In Canada, our universities and colleges rarely offer such perks to students regardless of athletic prowess. However, there are opportunities for students with special talent in athletics. Your high-school gym teacher or coach will be famliar with some. Others are available through specific universities and colleges. The listing below offers some of those available nationally.

1. **Bobby Bauer Memorial Hockey Awards.** One or more awards are made to students demonstrating proficiency in hockey who qualify for a full-time course at any Canadian university. Apply to: Bobby Bauer Memorial Foundation, P.O. Box 1283, Kitchener ON N2G 4G8.
2. **Health and Welfare Scholarship.** These athletic bursaries are based on need and athletic ability. Write for application forms to: Education Grants in Aid of Canadian Athletics, Fitness and Amateur Sport's Branch, Department of Health and Welfare, Journal Building, Ottawa ON K1A OX6.
3. **Canadian Golf Foundation.** This scholarship is valued at up to $4,000 per year. It recognizes excellence in scholastic achievement and in playing golf by young Canadian amateurs, as demonstrated by competition at the regional, provincial or

national level. Up to 24 of these scholarships are awarded each year. Deadline for applications is June 21. For application forms, see your school guidance counsellor or contact: Canadian Golf Foundation, Golf House, 1333 Dorval Dr., Oakville ON L6J 4Z3.

4. **Petro-Canada Olympic Torch Scholarship.** These awards, valued at $2,500, are available to both athletes and coaches. Application deadline is April 15. Contact: Canadian Olympic Association, 1600 James Naismith Dr., Ottawa ON K1B 5N4.
5. **Canadian Universities.** Canadian universities do offer some sports scholarships to athletic students to have them attend that university and play the sport in their area of expertise. However, sports scholarships in most Canadian universities and colleges are strictly regulated. Students receiving a sports scholarship at most Canadian universities and colleges must demonstrate academic competence as well as extraordinary sports ability. The Canadian Interuniversity Athletic Union (CIAU) regulates these sports at Canadian universities and colleges: men's/ women's basketball, cross-country running, soccer, swimming, track and field, volleyball; men's football, ice hockey, wrestling; and women's field hockey. The CIAU ensures that all awards must be for continuing students (second year and up), approved by the board of governors and administered by the university awards office. As well, booster clubs are not allowed to offer financial incentives to students.

Only Simon Fraser University in Burnaby, B.C., offers American-style sports scholarships as entrance awards to new students. Little money is available to college students who play intercollege sports and even that is tightly regulated. Students who wish to earn big bucks for playing sports in college will find such a prize "only in America."

Students who are highly accomplished in their sport and are members of a Canadian team that competes internationally and/or at the Olympic level should seek funding for their sports training through Sport Canada. The aim of the Athletic Assistance Program is to assist international-calibre athletes with expenses incurred during training and competition. More information is available from: Athletic Assistance Program, Place du Centre, 2nd Level, 200 Promenade du Portage, Hull PQ K1A 0X6.

Athletic coaches have been referring their star athletes to American colleges for years. This is still an effective way to land an athletic scholarship. Another effective way is to engineer an appearance at a relatively major tournament in your best sport at a center where a scout will be likely to notice your performance and offer a scholarship if you attend their post-secondary institution. Another method might be to explore the topic of *athletic scholarships* on the Internet. The Internet lists these as some suggestions concerning lines of approach:

- College Athletic Consulting Service (CACS) provides affordable, complete athletic and academic college scholarship services to both American and foreign students. Includes résumés and letters of introduction to educational institutions.
- College Athletic Placement Service provides personal attention and comprehensive athletic scholarship assistance. The postal address is: 16885 West Bernardo Dr., Ste. 275, Rancho Bernardo CA 92127; E-mail: webmaster@capsplacement.com
- College Athletic Scholarships has how-to video for athletes looking to obtain athletic scholarships.
- Graphic Sports Marketing offers a plan for high-school baseball players seeking college athletic scholarships.
- National Recruiting Network provides exposure, recruiting information and guidance throughout the recruiting process for both college-bound student-athletes and their parents.
- Scholar Athletic Matching Service (SAMS) locates colleges and scholarships for athletes.
- College Prospects of America Inc. has offices in Kelowna, North Vancouver, Calgary and Winnipeg. For approximately $650 (U.S.) the service will reproduce student profiles along with their coaches' reference and send them to American

universities in hopes of the student receiving scholarship offers from the universities. (Experience has shown that although most students receive some offers, they may well be from universities that do not offer the student's choice of program.)

Students and parents should check the reputation of any commercial services before they subscribe to them. Try contacting an American university directly to enquire as to whether they are familiar with the service and if it has a commendable reputation. The Department of Consumer Affairs might also be helpful.

CHAPTER TEN

Scholarships for specific groups

There are many scholarships set aside for students who are special in one or more ways. The challenge is for those who are eligible to find the opportunities. Among the scholarships available are those for First Nations Canadians, visible minorities and students with disabilities. Some scholarships with special criteria have been mentioned in the previous listings where there were too few to make a separate category. Look for those with criteria for certain ethnic backgrounds and languages.

FIRST NATIONS CANADIANS

1. **Casino Regina Scholarships.** This program awards two scholarships valued at $1,000 to entering and undergraduate university students and six $500 scholarships to students entering colleges and technical institutes. Preference is given to awarding at least one university scholarship and three college scholarships to aboriginal students. Contact your school guidance counsellor or Casino Regina Scholarship Committee, Vice-President, Corporate Affairs, 1880 Saskatchewan Dr., 3rd Floor, Regina SK S4P 0B2.
2. **CN Native Education Award Program.** Five awards, valued at $1,500 each, and renewable for up to four years are available to Inuit, Status Indian, Non-Status Indian or Métis students. Awards are based on a good academic record and financial need. Students must be interested in a career in the transportation industry. Application deadline is June 1. Contact: Employment Equity, Canadian National, 935 rue de la Gauchetiere St. W., 7th Floor, Montreal PQ H3B 2M9.

3. **Donald R. Simmons Memorial Scholarship.** This scholarship is offered to aboriginal students in Saskatchewan who will be pursuing post-secondary training, have a good academic standing and will not be winning a general proficiency award. Contact the school guidance counsellor or Student Financial Assistance, Saskatchewan Post-Secondary Education and Skills Training, 3085 Albert St., Regina SK S4P 3V7.
3. **Husky Native Awards Program.** This program offers scholarships, bursaries and possible summer employment to Native students who enroll at a university, technical school or community college in Canada to study accounting, business administration, chemistry, computer science, engineering, geology or geophysics (as well as other designated courses) that could lead to employment with Husky Oil. Application deadline is June 1. Contact: Native Affairs, Husky Oil, P.O. Box 6525, Station D, Calgary AB T2P 3G7.
4. **Imperial Oil Ltd. Native Educational Awards Program.** Four awards valued at $4,500 and renewable for up to four years are available to students who are entering a program relevant to the petroleum industry. Applicants must be of native ancestry and residents of British Columbia, Alberta, Saskatchewan, Northwest Territories or the Yukon for at least one year prior to applying. Financial need is important. Application deadline is June 15. Contact: Co-ordinator, Native Educational Awards Program, Human Resources Department, Imperial Oil, P.O. Box 2480, Station M237, 4th Ave SW, Calgary AB T2P 3M9.
5. **National Indian Brotherhood Assembly of First Nations' Heroes of Our Time.** First Nations citizens who have demonstrated exceptional athletic and academic ability, as well as a commitment to extracurricular activites, are eligible to apply for two awards valued at $2,000 each. Application deadline is June 15. Contact: Heroes of Our Time, The Assembly of First Nations, 55 Murray St., 5th Floor, Ottawa ON K1N 5M3.
6. **Petro-Canada Education Awards for Native Students.** Awards valued up to $5,000 a year and renewable for up to four years are available to students of Canadian Indian and Inuit ancestry. Students need to be entering a field related to the petroleum

industry and be in financial need. Contact: Employment Equity Office, Petro-Canada Inc., P.O. Box 2844, Calgary AB T2P 3E3.

7. **Royal Bank Native Student Awards.** Five awards valued at $4, 000 are available to status Indian, non-status Indian, Inuit or Métis students based on personal achievement, academic merit and financial need. For application forms see your guidance counsellor or contact: Student Awards & Financial Aid Office, Human Resources Office, Head Office, Royal Bank, 124 Front St. W., 7th Floor, Toronto ON M5J 2M2.
8. **Xerox Aboriginal Scholarships Program.** Four awards of $3,000 each are offered to status or non-status Indian, Metis, or Inuit students who are enrolled in a program with a significant content in information technology. Extracurricular activity and community leadership skills are important factors in this scholarship. Application deadline is June 15. Contact: Contributions Administrator, Corporate Affairs, Xerox Canada Ltd, 5650 Yonge St., North York ON M2M 4G7.

VISIBLE MINORITIES

1. **CanWest Global System Broadcasters of the Future Awards.** This award, valued at $4,000, is offered to a student of a self-identified visible minority who is entering a radio and television arts program or journalism. Contact: CanWest Global System - BFA, 81 Barber Greene Rd., Don Mills ON M3C 2A2.
2. **Harry Jerome Awards.** Five awards, valued at $2,000 each, and one award of $1,500 are available to students who have excelled in arts, athletics, and academics and who have made a commitment to the development of the black community. Awards are based on financial need. Contact: Harry Jerome Scholarships, 675 King St. W., Ste. 203, Toronto ON M5V 1M9.

For black students

There are hundreds of scholarships available for black students pursuing post-secondary education. Many guidance offices have a listing called "Directory of Black Scholarships." It's available directly from The Association of Black Employees of Ontario Hydro, P.O. Box 6205, Station A, Toronto ON M5W IP6

STUDENTS WITH PHYSICAL AND LEARNING DISABILITIES

A comprehensive list of opportunities and addresses of funding agencies can be found in *Funding Facts for Canadian Disabled Students*, by Susan Wheeler. This publication offers information regarding a wide variety of grants, scholarships and bursaries.

1. **CanWest Global System Broadcasters of the Future Awards.** This award is for students who have mobility impairment. The award, valued at up to $15,000 and a three- to four-month internship at the Global Television Network, is based on strong English-language communication skills. Students must be entering a radio and television arts or journalism program. Application deadline is May 31st. Contact CanWest Global System - BFA, 81 Barber Greene Rd., Don Mills ON M3C 2A2.
2. **Imasco Scholarship Fund for Disabled Students.** This scholarship provides funds of $2,000 annually for a minimum of five physically disabled students who may not be able to attend university because of additional expenses they might incur due to their disability. Contact: The Awards Division, Association of Universities and Colleges, 350 Albert St., Ste. 600, Ottawa ON K1P 1B1.
3. **National Access Awareness Week Student Awards Program.** A variable number of awards, valued at $3,500, are available to students with a disability who are pursuing a program with the intention of becoming an active member of Canada's labour force. Application deadline is March 15. Contact: Canadian Awards Program, International & Canadian Programs Division, Association of Universities & Colleges, 350 Albert St., Ste. 600, Ottawa ON K1R 1B1.

4. **The Carol Thomson Memorial Fund Scholarships for Students with Learning Disabilities.** These scholarships recognize students with a learning disability who, through effort and perseverance, are seeking to maximize their potential. This scholarship is worth $500 annually for one student. Application must be received by the Learning Disabilities Association no later than May 15. Contact: Carol Thomson Memorial Fund Scholarships, Maison Kildare House, 323 Chapel St., Ste. 200, Ottawa ON K1N 7Z2.
5. **Telephone Pioneers of America.** This scholarship is designed to help students with disabilities to enter the post-secondary institute of their choice. Application deadline is August 1. Contact: Saskatchewan Chapter 59, Telephone Pioneers of America, 2121 Saskatchewan Dr., 2nd Floor, Regina SK S4P 3Y2.

INTERNATIONAL STUDENTS

1. **Knights of Columbus Pro Deo and Pre Patria Scholarships.** This organization provides $1,500 scholarships for one year, renewable for each year of undergraduate study for up to four years. Successful candidates must be entering their first year at a university and the son or daughter of a Knights of Columbus member. Applications must be submitted by May 1 to: Director of Scholarship Aid, Knights of Columbus, P.O. Box 1670, New Haven CT 06507-0901.

Ethnic scholarships

Many ethnic and national organizations provide scholarships for students whose families are members of their groups. There are, for example, the Da Vinci Scholarships for students of Italian descent and scholarships from Icelandic clubs for students with Icelandic heritage. For information on these types of scholarships, check with your family's social club or place of worship.

CORPORATE SCHOLARSHIPS

Many companies offer scholarship programs to the children of their employees. The list below is not exhaustive, so be sure to check with your parents.

Ordinarily, the criteria and application forms are available through the personnel office where your parent works. Have them ask at the office about this. Unfortunately, these scholarships are usually limited to *dependent* children. If you've been living away from home or are over 25, it's unlikely these will benefit you.

ABB Canada
ABT Building Products Canada Limited
Abitibi-Consolidated Ltd.
AgrEvo Canada Inc.
Allied Signal Canada Inc.
Amoco Canada Petroleum Company Limited
Apotex Inc.
Asten Canada Inc.
Avenor Inc.
Anevor Maritimes
Ball Packaging Products Canda, Inc.
BASF Canada Inc.
Beaver Lumber Company Limited
Bell Canada
Bell Helicopter TEXTRON
Bristol-Myers Squibb Canada Inc.
Browning-Ferris Industries, Inc.
Business Development Bank of Canada
CGC Inc.
CIBC Wood Gundy Securities Inc.
Canadian National
Canadian Pacific Forest Products
Canadian Reynolds Metals Company Ltd.
Cargill Limited
Chevron Canada Resources
Colgate-Palmolive Canada Inc.
La Compagnie Miniere Quebec Cartier

Conoco Canada Limited
Consumers Packaging Inc.
Corby Distilleries Limited
Cytec Canada Inc.
Department of Transport Canada
Dresser Industries, Inc.
E.B. Eddy Forest Products
Electro-Federation Canada
Equifax Canada
Framatome Connectors Canada Inc
Gaz Metropolitan
GenCorp Vehicle Sealing
Gilbey Canada Inc.
HOJ Management Inc.
Hoechst & Celanese Canada Inc.
ICI Canada Inc.
Ingersoll-Rand Canada Inc.
International Nickel Co. of Canada
International Union of Bricklayers and Allied Craftsworkers
Iron Ore Company of Canada
The Island Telephone Company Ltd.
James Richardson & Sons, Limited
Johnson & Higgins Ltd.
Kraft Canada Inc.
Lafarge Canada Inc.
Lombard Canada Ltd.
Macmillan Bathurst Inc.
Maritime Telegraph and Telephone Company
MDS Nordion
Merck Frosst Canada Inc.
Metropolitan Life Insurance Company
Mobil Chemical Canada, Ltd.
Mobil Oil Canada
Molson Breweries
The Molson Companies Limited
Monenco AGRA Inc.
Motorola Canada Limited

Nabisco Ltd.
Navistar International Corporation of Canada
The New Brunswick Telephone Company, Limited
Norfolk Southern Corporation
Novacor Chemicals LTD
NOVA Corporation
Owens-Corning Foundation Inc.
PPG Canada Inc.
Pepsi-Cola Beverages Canada
Pfizer Canada Inc.
Procor Ltd.
Proctor & Gamble Inc.
Quebec Telephone
RJR-Macdonald Inc.
Phone-Poulenc Canada Inc.
Rockwell International of Canada Ltd.
Rothmans, Benson & Hedges Inc.
Russel Metals Inc.
Sara Lee Corporation
Scott Paper Limited
Sears Canada Inc.
Shaklee Canada Inc.
St. Laurent Paperboard Inc.
St. Lawrence Seaway Authority
Standen's Limited
State Farm Mutual Automobile Insurance Company
Stone Container (Canada) Inc.
Suncor Energy
Tamrock Loaders
Telebec Itee
Telesat Canada
TransCanada PipeLines
Twinpak Inc.
UAP Inc.
Ultramar Canada Inc.
Unilever Canada Limited
Unisys Canada Inc.

United Distillers Canada Inc.
Universal Terminals Inc.
Versa Services Ltd.
Warner-Lambert Canada Inc.
Westinghouse Canada Inc.
Weston Bakeries Ltd.
Weyerhaeuser Canada Ltd.
Weyerhaeuser Canada Limited - Grande Prairie Operations
Whirlpool Foundation
Wrigley Canada Inc.
Wyeth-Ayerst Canada Inc
Xerox Canada Inc.
Zeneca Agro

CHAPTER ELEVEN

American scholarships

Canadian students seeking to further their education in the United States have the option of applying for both academic and athletic scholarships in that country as well as Canada. Students considering applying for scholarships in the United States for either reason should realize a few facts.

- You will usually be required to take an SAT (Scholastic Aptitude Test) as measurement of academic qualifications and suitability for attending university.
- Attending college/university in the United States does not ensure that you will be allowed to remain there after graduation to seek employment. This fact may not be significant at the outset of university training, but may become quite vital after four years, especially if lasting relationships and friendships have been formed.
- Be sure to understand all the terms of every scholarship that is offered.
- Be wary of a scholarship promised to you by a booster club member. There should not be any secret scholarships.
- Check out any university personally before accepting the scholarship or committing yourself to attend. A good brochure or recruiter may mask a mediocre school.
- Travel to and from a distant university can eat up most of that lucrative scholarship. Think about the total financial situation carefully.
- Few college athletes ever become professional athletes. Are you ready for the extra challenge of study, dedicating every

waking hour to travel, practice and playing a sport, as well as the loneliness of separation from family and friends?

Many prestigious universities in the United States have extraordinary tuition and living expenses, especially in terms of Canadian dollars. An Ivy League tuition of $25,000 (U.S.) and living expenses of $10,000 a year are not uncommon figures. Nonetheless, the more prestigious schools have healthy endowments and big scholarship funds to help relatively poor (and in U.S. dollars, almost all Canadians are) but high-achieving students. Full-tuition scholarships are not uncommon. Packages of scholarships, part-time work and loans will often cover all your obvious costs.

Ordinarily, you'll receive scholarship application forms with American college application forms. If not, ask for them. Your parents will also have to complete a statement of income and financial resources.

Many American states and American protectorates have compiled lists of available scholarships and bursaries for students in their jurisdiction. Contact the department of education at the particular state capital to see if a list is available for you.

Many state scholarships and bursaries are available only to high-school graduates from that particular state; however, foreign students sometimes become eligible after a year of residence. Check the rules carefully. American private colleges have many more scholarships available than do Canadian schools. Lists of these will ordinarily be provided when you apply for admission and request financial aid.

CHAPTER TWELVE

Preparing to win the scholarship

The previous chapters have been dedicated to helping you increase your scholarship awareness. This is the first and perhaps most important step to follow in your pursuit of scholarships and financial assistance. However, if that is the only step that you and your parents take, your financial assistance will remain at zero. There's much more work to be done before you can win scholarships. In order to win scholarships, scholars must be prepared to invest:

- sustained awareness
- patience
- effort
- courage

Sustained awareness. Scholarship awareness needs to begin early in a supportive home and school environment where parents, students and teachers have high expectations of each other. Each group should expect the other to achieve their personal best, from providing excellent education to thoroughly researching opportunities.

Schools can be tremendous scholarship boosters. They can salute student achievement in many ways. Some annually host a showcase of student achievement, a recognition evening late in fall after most awards and scholarships have been announced. It is an opportunity to congratulate all students on their efforts and personal bests achieved over the year. Some schools hang large collages of the annual award winners in the hallways along with printouts of their accomplishments.

Career education classrooms often sport a scroll of current scholarship winners and their winnings. Classes from grades 9 to 12, using that classroom, might seize the opportunity to discuss the requirements of new and traditional scholarships. A frequent question after a new scholarship winner has been posted might be "What would I have to do to win that scholarship?" All scholarship winners, their pictures and their accomplishments can be published in the local newspaper. These announcements could be clipped from the newspaper and kept in a photo album as a record of the achievements of students, staff and school.

Parents, educators, students and the community are indispensable team members to help you win a scholarship. They should be ever on the alert to new scholarship opportunities, clipping information from magazines and tipping the career education department about new scholarships initiated by service clubs and organizations. In the last five years, at least twice as many new scholarships have been established as old ones discontinued.

Steps towards sustained awareness

1. Use this book to find the listed sources of money for which you are eligible.
2. Check with the awards offices of the post-secondary institutions of your choice.
3. Check with other businesses, organizations, labor unions, professional associations, etc. that may have unadvertised scholarships. Particularly check with organizations of which your parents are members.
4. Additional sources can be found in the closest public library. Check the *Canadian Directory of Foundations and Granting Agencies Sources of Funds Index* as well as the awards publication released by Association of Universities and Colleges of Canada (AUCC).
5. Join a scholarship club in your school.
6. Ask for advice from your school's guidance counsellor. If there's a choice, go to the counsellor with the best track record.

Patience The secret to sustaining your interest in applying for scholarships is to attend carefully to one scholarship at a time. By your second and third applications, you will be surprised at how much required information carries over from one scholarship to the next. You will also be surprised at how much you learn about your special skills, interests and abilities when supplying the supporting documentation for a scholarship application. You will discover previously unnoticed traits about your character. In addition, you'll find this effort to have been a useful process when it comes time to sell your skills on a job application form. When one application is complete, mail it. Then forget about it and whether or not you will win; begin concentrating on the next.

Effort Applying for scholarships requires work. If you are lazy or disorganized, completing scholarship applications can become a major stress and source of frustration. Many applications require not only that you complete a form and write an essay, but often ask for three letters of reference as well as a transcript of marks.

Interpersonal skills come into play here. It is important that you think carefully about who could provide the most relevant and positive letter of reference. Who can express observations about you in a meaningful, concise manner? Who will fully realize the depth of this task and be motivated to showcase your skills to your advantage? Be sure to ask those referees for their letters in plenty of time so that they have time to fully consider what material they wish to include. Be considerate. Supply those people with the criteria of the scholarship so they can best highlight the skills and abilities that make you a natural winner of the scholarship. Give them a copy of your involvement checklist too, to help their writing along.

Organization becomes a key to successful scholarship applications. It helps reduce the pressure of deadlines, keeps you feeling "in control" and positive about your tasks. Your mood is reflected in your response to questions. Be sure to keep sufficiently on top of tasks so that you have time to have someone proofread your forms and essays. Nothing robs applicants of scholarships more quickly than spelling mistakes, awkward sentence structure and understated involvement and accomplishments.

Courage Applying for scholarships is not for the "lily-livered." There are few guarantees in scholarship endeavors. Applicants need to be aware that it takes courage to apply for 5, 10 or 15 scholarships and receive rejection slips for many or all of those applications.

However, applicants also need to be aware that each year several scholarships are not awarded because no one applies for them. You can never estimate what your competition for any scholarship will be, so if you are eligible at all, apply, apply, apply!

FREQUENTLY ASKED QUESTIONS

1. **Do I have to be at the top of my class to win scholarships?**

   No. Most scholarships award students with averages of 70 percent or better, but marks are only part, not all, of the criteria for many scholarships. Often, school and community involvement, as well as a candidate's ability to achieve goals and overcome physical and mental disabilities, are considered.

2. **Do students from larger schools have a better chance of winning scholarships?**

   No, again. In fact, students from smaller schools have a better chance. Those students not only have the opportunity but, by necessity, often fulfill roles as president of the student body, volleyball captain, editor of the newspaper and yearbook, and several other leadership roles simultaneously. There is often no one else to do the jobs. In larger schools, it is likely that those positions would be distributed among more students.

3. **What if you are not sure what you want to do but you still want to apply?**

   Apply anyway. However, be prepared to perhaps sacrifice a scholarship if, eventually, you choose a career that is not included in that scholarship's criteria. For example, 4-H and the Saskatchewan Wheat Pool offer scholarships to students entering agriculture. If you are awarded a scholarship but do not enter the School of Agriculture, you will be asked to forfeit the scholarship.

4. **What are my scholarship opportunities if I choose to attend an out-of-province post-secondary school?**

Be advised that if you choose to attend an out-of-province post-secondary school, you narrow your scholarship opportunities. Some clubs, organizations, governments and colleges offer scholarships solely to residents of their province attending school in that province. Others, such as Augustana University College in Camrose, Alberta, offer scholarship incentives especially for students from out-of-province. Some students from the United States and England have chosen Canadian universities to complete their masters and doctorates, at least partially because of the scholarships offered to them as foreign post-graduate students. It is always wise to query any post-secondary institution about its scholarship programs with the initial request for information about academic programs.

5. **Can I enhance my opportunities by striving to be involved in school and community activities?**

Absolutely. Involvement in any positive, supportive activitiy that demonstrates that you are aware of others and their needs speaks volumes about your character. Such character traits make scholarship donors see you in a strong light - a solid investment in the future, a good risk, a certain winner, the type of person our world needs more of. As a result, the donors are more likely to see the applicant as deserving a thousand extra dollars to help finance college. The stress of financing an education is somewhat reduced and the applicant begins to feel empowered - other people and organizations are viewing the applicant as a good bet and an individual with potential. A little moral support always feels good, too.

Many school guidance counsellors advise students to have a few hundred hours of community service experience to strengthen their scholarship and university applications. Often you're not eligible for a scholarship unless you have this background and a record of school involvement as well.

6. **Should I have to pay money to apply for a scholarship?**

Never. If you are required to send money to apply for a scholarship, it is likely a scam. But some scholarship "services" will provide you with a scholarship list customized for you. It might or might not be worth the $30–$50 they charge.

- Get involved today for the scholarships and jobs of tomorrow. Start in grade 10 or sooner.
- Even if you do not win any scholarships, applying is not time or effort wasted. You can use a lot of the same information when applying to a post-secondary institute or when applying for a job. It's a good start on your résumé.
- Be sure to list the awards and scholarships that you have won on your résumé. A former student believes that listing them on her job résumé was at least partially responsible for the nine job offers she received following her graduation.

NOTHING BREEDS SUCCESS LIKE SUCCESS

The following case studies are true. They are used with the permission of their subjects to illustrate some of the diverse types of students who are deserving scholarship recipients.

CASE STUDY 1

Background: Sarah had always been a high-achieving student. During grade 10, however, her focus changed to more social than academic. Much time was spent working at a part-time job rather than on extracurricular or volunteer activities. Her marks were good, but not representative of her ability. However, at her part-time job as a gas jockey, she met a person who made a significant impression and led Sarah to explore the possibility of a future as a petroleum engineer. Sarah became committed to a goal for her future. Over the next two years, her marks began to reflect her true potential. Even though she continued to work many hours at her job, her grades climbed.

Achievement: In May 1992, Sarah won the Morgan Hydrocarbons Scholarship for students from her school entering the hydrocarbon industry. In September 1992, she was the recipient of a Canada

Scholarship worth $2,000 annually. This scholarship was discontinued during the second year of her course. However, in September 1993, she was awarded the Cactus Drilling Scholarship from Northern Alberta Institute of Technology.

Value: $1,000 $2,000 $500

Outcome: Sarah graduated as a petroleum engineering technologist in April 1994. She found immediate employment with Mobil Oil in Rainbow Lake, Alberta. She is now married and raising a son. In the future, she plans to re-enter the petroleum industry using her post-secondary training and education.

CASE STUDY 2

Background: Jim was often called a below-average student because of his lack of academic motivation. Over the years he received some small-group instruction in the special-education program in conjunction with a regular classroom program. Extra help at home was not possible. Jim repeated grade 6. Over the next few years, perhaps as a result of seeing positive results from intense effort in sports and positive peer influence, Jim learned that intense effort in studying might also have positive results. By grade 12, Jim at last became an honor student.

Achievement: Jim won the Delta Co-op Scholarship for most deserving student in his class.

Value: $500

Outcome: Jim plans to be a physical education teacher. He is currently enrolled in fourth year of kinesiology at the University of Saskatchewan.

CASE STUDY 3

Background: Joelle had always shown great academic promise. Her achievement was consistent despite one parents' personal problems and a relatively low family income. Joelle's gentle, loving nature is coupled with the drive to do well in all her endeavors. She was active in the church choir and children's liturgy. In the community, Joelle was a candystriper at a seniors' home and participated in a self-help group for children of chemically dependent parents. She is a talented organist, who took lessons, taught lessons to children of the community and shared her talent as an entertainer at community functions.

Achievement: Joelle was nominated for and the recipient of a Terry Fox Humanitarian Award.

Value: $4,000 annually for 4 years

Outcome: Joelle has completed a commerce degree from the University of Saskatchewan with a major in marketing. During each summer break she worked for the Saskatchewan Wheat Pool, gaining experience and additional funds to finance her education. Joelle is now employed full-time with the Saskatchewan Wheat Pool.

CASE STUDY 4

Background: Jodi was an average student who suffered from mild epilepsy as a result of a minor birth defect. Although termed a special-needs student, she consistently overachieved - especially in mathematics - thanks to extreme determination and hard work. Jodi's positive attitude and courage made her a winner long before grade 12 when scholarship recognition became available.

Achievement: Jodi was the winner of the Winterhawk Scholarship for diligence.

Value: $700

Outcome: Jodi was initally interested in pursuing a career in the medical profession. She was accepted and began a diploma course in nursing at the Saskatchewan Institute of Arts & Science Technology at Kelsey Institute in Saskatoon. Following a seizure, she was required to discontinue her studies. She then went to London, Ontario, twice for surgery as a possible cure for her disability. She continues to have fleeting periods of confusion, but is enrolled at Lakeland College in business administration.

CASE STUDY 5

Background: Kyle was a student with excellent intentions, who worked very hard at his part-time job. His high-school drama performances were a priority in his life, but carrying out his daily school work was often a struggle. Kyle achieved average marks. His place of employment, a well-known service-station chain, offers back-to-school scholarships at the high school, college and university levels to students who apply and write an essay on a designated topic. Coached by his parents and personally interested in the boost that winning a scholarship would give him, Kyle asked for the advice of his career education teacher in the project. The personal information regarding his life and the special qualities of his place of work were not a problem. Following his advisor's suggestion, Kyle used a CD-ROM for information for his essay. Kyle summarized and conferred. His boss wrote a reference and Kyle mailed the completed application ahead of the deadline.

Achievement: Besides the personal satisfaction from completing a task that required organization, consultation, research, soul-searching, and language skills, Kyle also won a PetroCan Back-to-school scholarship.

Value: $400

Goal: Kyle continues since graduation to work in a management-training capacity at a PetroCan service outlet.

- Apply for many scholarships - even those you don't think you will get. You can't win what you don't apply for.
- Always make rough copies and think *positively*.
- Never throw any work you have done (essays, letters, etc.) for scholarships away. It may be helpful or reusable in other scholarships you apply for.

CHAPTER THIRTEEN

Worksheets

STUDENT WORKSHEET

Preliminary checklist (answer yes or no)

_____Would scholarship funds assist you to continue your post-secondary training?

_____Does opportunity intrigue you?

_____Are you prepared to work, think and concentrate?

_____Are you reasonably confident in your abilities?

_____Are you courageous, motivated and optimistic?

_____Are you innovative, committed and organized?

_____Are you imaginative, ambitious and determined?

_____Can you work collaboratively with teachers and parents?

_____Are you willing to dedicate time and effort to preparing yourself for applying for scholarships from grade 9 through high school?

_____Can you represent yourself objectively in writing, highlighting your positive attributes?

_____Are you willing to apply for a scholarship knowing that you may not win?

If your answer to four or more of these questions is yes, then get started. Begin by taking these steps:

1. Get informed. Research, obtain forms, read and analyze, make notes, concentrate and discuss with parents and teachers.
2. Plan. Help yourself, and referees, by completing a student involvement checklist (on p. 106) as you proceed through high school. List the scholarships that you wish to apply for in the

order of the application deadline (form follows in this chapter).

3. Read and reread the criteria until you can almost recite them in your sleep. Keeping the criteria in mind will help keep you on task, slanting each of your answers towards the scholarship objectives.
4. Begin by filling in the easy parts of forms.
5. Think about referees, striving to find a variety of sources (teachers, employers, volunteer supervisors).
6. Request transcripts from your school office.
7. Think again about letters of reference. Discuss possible options with parents and teachers.
8. Begin to formulate any needed essays using an outline. It is an advantage to do essays on computer so that they can be easily edited, expanded and adapted for use in other scholarship applications. Of course the greatest advantage is that the essays can be saved!
9. Request letters of reference **at least two months prior** to the date the application is due. Supply your referees with a student involvement checklist and the criteria of the scholarship so that they know what aspects of your character to address.
10. Ask a parent or teacher to proofread any essays and make suggestions.
11. Keep all applications in one place in your room or office.
12. As you receive your application forms and begin to complete them, address the envelope that you will use to mail it. On the flap, in pencil, note the deadline and documents that are needed. As you receive those documents, erase that note until the package is complete.
13. Mail the application two weeks before the deadline. Using registered mail is preferred - especially if you're close to the due date.

Extra tips to help win scholarships

1. You must fit the criteria or be an outstanding applicant who closely fits the criteria.
2. Type responses on forms whenever possible. If you do not have access to a typewriter, then print the answers in *black* ink.
3. Highlight your achievements without bragging. You need to believe you are a winner before you can win. This is not the time to wilt behind modesty.
4. Achieve your best in school. Some scholarships are based on grade 11 final marks. It is too late to leave studying until your finals and then see what happens!

AIDS TO HELP YOU APPLY FOR SCHOLARSHIPS

Scholarships and bursaries I wish to apply for
(preliminary form)

Name	**Deadline**

Scholarships and bursaries I wish to apply for

Use this form to reorganize scholarships and bursaries according to chronological deadline dates.

Name ____________________

Address ____________________

Have Form ☐ Need Form ☐ Deadline ____________

Name ____________________

Address ____________________

Have Form ☐ Need Form ☐ Deadline ____________

Name ____________________

Address ____________________

Have Form ☐ Need Form ☐ Deadline ____________

Name ____________________

Address ____________________

Have Form ☐ Need Form ☐ Deadline ____________

Name ____________________

Address ____________________

Have Form ☐ Need Form ☐ Deadline ____________

Name ____________________

Address ____________________

Have Form ☐ Need Form ☐ Deadline ____________

Scholarships and bursaries I am applying for

Use these pages to duplicate for yourself as an organizational aid (check off as completed).

Example

1. Terry Fox Feb. 1 $4,000/year

___Referee #1 Mr. T. K.

___Referee #2 Amber M.

___Referee #3 Robert A.

___Nomination letter

___Transcript of marks

___Mail by Jan. 23

___Thank-you card to referees

___Photocopy completed form for reference

___Give referees information they need

____

____

2.______ ______ ________ ___________________

____

____

____

____

____

____

____

____

____

____

3.______ ______ _________ ________________________

4.______ ______ _________ ________________________

PARENT WORKSHEET

Preliminary checklist (answer yes or no)

_____Are you intensely interested in helping your son or daughter to capitalize on opportunities?

_____Do you see yourself as an ally in your child's quest for opportunity?

_____Are you willing to devote a few hours a month to developing strategies and wordings for scholarship applications, and remembering details of your son's or daughter's community, extracurricular and academic involvement?

_____Can you read, proofread and analyze information?

_____Can you concentrate, communicate and collaborate?

_____Can you help you son or daughter to research and search tirelessly for opportunity?

_____Can you motivate, build spirit, encourage, provide moral support and provide backup when frustration comes?

If your answer to most of the above questions is yes, then you are in a position to help.

Students applying for scholarships are much more likely to win awards when they elicit parental support and involvement. It has been proven that parents are invaluable as resources prompting students to recall their involvement in community activities and projects, special achievements and daily services that set them apart from their peers. You can help them remember paper routes, entertainment, choir and band participation, routine care for the elderly and the very young. Many parents are educated enough to be excellent proofreaders. Besides that, once students have captured their parents' interest by including them in their goals, parents often take on a new respect for the student and the student's mission in life. Who knows, parents may even begin their own search for scholarship opportunities.

Begin by taking these steps:

1. Get informed: research, obtain forms, read and analyze, make notes, concentrate, and discuss goals and opportunities with your student and his or her teachers.
2. Plan.
3. Offer to proofread and suggest areas of involvement that the student may have forgotten or neglected to highlight.
4. Support and encourage - applying for scholarships is difficult and sometimes discouraging work, especially when coupled with the rigors of other student activities such as essays, exams, hockey tournaments and music festivals. Students often begin to wonder whether they are really special and deserving of recognition. Many begin the process and never finish. This is where the supportive parent and teacher can provide a firm shoulder to lean on. Offer your assistance when needed.
5. Research and search for new scholarship opportunities. Think about where you work and the organizations to which you belong.
6. Keep stamps on hand.

SCHOLARSHIP COACH WORKSHEET

Preliminary checklist (answer yes or no)

____Are you committed to assisting your students to capitalize on their opportunity?

____Are you a promoter, facilitator and motivator?

____Do you inspire trust?

____Do you demonstrate patience, courage, and never-ending determination?

____Do you demand your students' and your own best efforts?

____Can you communicate "hope"?

____Do you model a strong and positive work ethic?

____Can you "see clearly" the application criteria of the scholarship?

____Can you concentrate on each student's dreams and schemes, even in the shower?

____Do you believe that your class has winners?

____Do you enjoy researching, organizing and analyzing?

____Do you take the time to discover the traits that make each student unique and special in his or her own way?

These are some of the most important traits necessary in an educator who hopes to inspire students to apply for and win scholarships. If you can answer yes to most of them, you will become a super scholarship coach! According to Michael Howell in *Winning Scholarships*, "the coach must have the ability to communicate with young people and know how to motivate them.... An important part of the job of the scholarship coach is to connect the right student with the right opportunity."

Make no mistake, a scholarship coach in the school is as important to the prospect of students winning scholarships as a good football coach is to the probability of a football team winning football games. Go for the gold - your students will not let you down.

CHAPTER FOURTEEN

Sample questions from scholarship applications

Many scholarship applications call for a personal essay or essay-type answers to a set of questions. This is your opportunity to showcase the special skills and background you have that make you deserving of a scholarship. Your answers have to balance what you have done in high school and the community with the criteria of the scholarship. For instance, volunteering at a seniors' center would be a good response for a scholarship requiring community service, but not as important if applying for an athletic scholarship. The better your answers fit, the more likely you are to win.

Remember the basics

- Fit your answer to the scholarship criteria.
- Use active verbs.
- Provide details of what you actually did.
- Always check your spelling and punctuation.
- Use black ink.
- Do not use liquid paper.

Here are a few questions often found on scholarship applications with sample answers.

SAMPLE SCHOLARSHIP QUESTIONS

1. List *six* tasks you have performed that, taken together, describe your character.

Example

- Completed my Bronze Medallion and Bronze Cross in Royal Lifesaving.
- Coached minor softball for eight year-olds.
- Volunteered to teach pre-beginners in CanSkate Figure Skating in our town.
- Participated in Missoula Children's Theatre.
- Volunteered each year to sort, box and deliver clothing during the fall clothing drive that my church conducts annually.
- Received *Top Player* award in Midget Hockey in 1999.

2. Describe your volunteer community service.

Example

For the past two years I have been a member of my church choir. This involves singing at regular Sunday masses as well as weddings, anniversaries and funerals. On average, being in the choir occupies one to two hours of my time each week.

For the past two years I have been candystriping at our local health center. Candystriping involves doing various activities, such as playing bingo and Yahtzee with the elderly. This occupies two hours of my time each week.

3. Describe your volunteer activities at your high school, college and/or university.

Example

For the past year I have been a student volunteer in elementary classes in my school. Student volunteers do such things as helping with math, spelling and reading, as well as making billboards. This takes about an hour of my time a week.

For the past two years I have been a room representative on the SRC. Being on the council involves working at the school canteen and working on the school milk program for about two hours per week.

Start filling these sample scholarship questions out in Grade 9 or 10. When you begin applying for scholarships in grade 12, the information will be organized and complete and you won't miss recording some of the attributes that make you a natural candidate for the scholarship.

4. Which of your volunteer activities have you found to be of most worth to you and others – and why?

Example

I found candystriping to be the most satisfying community work. I really enjoyed getting to know some of the elderly people in my community. It is gratifying to know that I am helping people who have trouble helping themselves.

5. What influence has your volunteer community service had over your choice of career?

Example

My experience with community service will have a very direct effect on my intended vocation as a physiotherapist. Candystriping has given me a taste of what working with disabled and elderly people will be like. As well, helping with children's liturgy has given me the opportunity to work with children, which I will do as a physiotherapist.

6. a) List the major community activities in which you have taken part in the past three years and your role in these activities.

Example

Activity	**Role**	**Year**
Community baseball	Pitcher	Summers 1997, 1998
Candystriping	Caregiver	1995-96/1996-97
Volunteer at museum	Groundskeeper	Summer 1998

T-ball coach	Coached team of kids ages 8 and 9	Summers 1997, 1998, 1999
Volunteer entertainer	Juggled at St. Joseph's Integrated Health Care Centre	four times in 1998
Youth diocesan retreat team	Facilitator	1996–present

b) Select one of these and discuss why you became involved, how your community benefited and what you gained from the experience.

Example

I became involved with the Youth Diocesan Retreat Team because, like many youth today, I was struggling with my faith. I felt uncomfortable sharing my faith and beliefs with others and I wanted to be able to share my struggle with others so that they could also become more comfortable as I was hoping to. Young people at the retreat learned that they were not the only ones questioning their faith. They realized it was all right to question; they weren't to be condemned. From the experience, I gained a whole new perspective on my religion.

7. Describe your volunteer community activities here. (*Notice that the material requested here is a reiteration of the material requested elsewhere, but asked in a slightly different format.)*

8. List the extracurricular activities you were involved in during the past three years.

Example

Activity	**Year**
SRC co-president	1998-99
Senior girls volleyball team (captain in 1999)	1997-99
Senior badminton	1996-99
Track & field team	1996-99
Yearbook committee (Editor in 1998)	1997-99

b) Select one of these and discuss why you became involved and what experience you gained.

Example

I became involved with the SRC because I wanted to help promote school spirit. I also wanted to try to make realities of the many ideas I had for our school. From being on the SRC I learned that things only get accomplished when hard work is involved and that you can only get a task done when you have the support of your SRC and the student body.

9. Describe your participation in student activities, highlighting the variety and type of activities, including offices held. (Exclude volunteer service previously mentioned.)

Example

For the past year I have been on my school yearbook committee. The yearbook committee does various fundraising activities, prepares copy and takes photographs for the school's yearbook. We meet at least once a week and much more often as the deadline approaches and most of the material is turned in.

For the past four years, I have been in the school choir. This involves practicing at noon hours and doing recitals at school functions.

10. Describe any awards and recognition that you have received, mentioning both academic and other awards.

Example

a) Academic	Mathematics Competition Winner	1998, 1999
	Academic Award	1997, 1998
	Honor Roll	1997, 1998, 1999

b) Other

11. Athletic background: List your best personal accomplishments (maximum of five) within the last five years in team or individual sports, identifying the competition or event, your involvement and results. (Indicate dates.)

Example

a) Jupiter School Soccer Team

- Timbutu division competition
- goalie
- Jupiter won championship, 1999

b) Mars Handball Team

- provincial competition
- doubles player
- fifth in provincial competition, 1998

12. What benefits do you consider that you have derived from your participation in organized amateur athletics or your personal fitness program?

Example

I feel that my personal fitness program has afforded me the physical and mental stability and courage to meet life's challenges in a capable and controlled manner. Participation in sports offers a release from tension and pressure, as well as a feeling of well-being. Participation in team sports offers an opportunity to interact with my peers in a positive way and meet new people while competing with others who value sports.

13. What particular personal obstacles have you been required to overcome while in pursuit of your academic, extracurricular, amateur sport, fitness, health and voluntary community service endeavors?

Example

I was born prematurely and with muscular dystrophy so that when I began to participate in the Early Childhood Intervention Program at school I could not walk or talk. I underwent several operations to help me gain control of my hands, feet and legs, and within a couple of years, I began to walk, talk and write, as well as work on the computer. My teacher aide worked and exercised with me every day, always believing that I could learn like other children. Each year I progressed with the children of my age, joining in some activities in the classroom each day. By grade 4, I was participating in the classroom lessons with other children. Catching up was difficult, but with the help of my family, teacher aide, teachers and friends, I became a regular classroom student. They convinced me that I had learned even faster than they had and that gave me courage and determination to work even harder. Sometimes I found I could even help other students, especially those who were having difficulty believing that success was within their power. That work ethic prepared me for the challenge of high school and helped me to excel so that today I am scholarship material.

14. Outline any special circumstances that may have affected your involvement in activities or that might have a bearing on your eligibility for this scholarship.

Example

I am a member of a single-parent family of Native ancestry. Although my ancestry hasn't had any direct effect on my performance, I feel that being a member of a single-parent family has often limited my participation in volunteer activities. As I became older, I have found it increasingly necessary to hold a part-time job to finance activities that I wished to participate in, such as for school tours, track and field equipment, trips, entry fees, sports costs and education fees. Often I must choose my part-time work instead of training for track and field or working on a volunteer activity after school, such as yearbook-committee tasks.

Remember:

- The first scholarship you apply for is the hardest - gathering all the information on your academic and extracurricular activities, finding references, etc. Each one you apply for after that will be easier because you have most of the information and strategies in place.
- Start early - that way you have plenty of time for essays, etc.
- Do not be intimidated if you do not have a 90+ average. Extracurricular activities, such as athletics, volunteer work and part-time jobs, are as important as your academic achievements when applying for scholarships. There are also scholarships offered to students from specific geographical areas, students who are members of a specific organization (i.e., 4-H), agency (i.e., credit union), ethnic group (i.e., aboriginal), or education-equity group (i.e., Aboriginal people, persons with disabilities, visible minorities and women).

CHAPTER FIFTEEN

How to help someone write a reference for you

Most scholarships (and many applications for admission) require letters of reference. Sometimes these are sent separately to an address supplied; sometimes you're asked to send the letters with your scholarship application form.

In either event, you'll need one, two or three letters of reference from people who know you and are not in your family. The best combination is usually one letter from a teacher, one letter from someone in the community and one letter from a person of some stature who has known you for some period of time. Only you can determine who'd be best to write your letters of reference. Think about these possibilities:

- teachers
- coaches
- leaders of local organizations (Kinsmen, Rotary club, political groups)
- church officials
- employers
- neighbors and family friends

A letter of reference is always written on the letterhead of the organization to which your referee belongs or on a form provided by the scholarship organization. It takes a referee up to two hours to prepare a good letter of reference, so don't ask casually or unnecessarily for a letter. On the other hand, once a letter is written, it's easy to use the **same letter** for many different purposes, especially if the letter is done on a computer.

You should help your referee to write an effective letter. Here's how:

1. Tell the referee to expect questions like the following on the scholarship application form.

- How long have you known the candidate?
- What area of the candidate's performance are are you most familiar with?

  a) Academic
  b) Athletic
  c) Volunteer community service
  d) All of the above

- How would you rate this applicant compared to the young people you have dealt with over the years?

Please consider voluntary community service, perseverance in sport and fitness, academic standing and courage in overcoming obstacles.

2. If the scholarship application does not provide specific questions for the referee to answer, suggest that your referee use a general formula such as:

I have known ________ since _________.

He/she has been involved in numerous volunteer activities both in the school and in the community (elaborate on these).

He/she is also involved in the following student activities (describe these).

Academically, he/she has——— (describe).

Athletically, he/she has——— (describe).

As well as being strong academically and athletically, he/she has also had to overcome personal difficulties including——— (describe).

In conclusion, I think ______ is worthy of this scholarship because

——— (describe). I am pleased to recommend _____ for this scholarship.

Sincerely,
Referee's name
Referee's occupation

3. Give your referee a copy of your student involvement checklist or a copy of something that summarizes your academic, athletic, personal and voluntary endeavors. Assure your referee that your reference need not be longer than one page.

- Don't be afraid to ask for reference letters or feel that you are imposing.
- If you need three letters of reference and one referee is someone busy or living far away, ask four people to do the references. It is convenient to have a bit of leeway if someone does not return their letter of reference to you in time.
- Always keep an extra copy of letters of reference. If you have only one copy left, make an extra and get it signed.
- If you really like a particular reference, ask the person who wrote it if you can use it for another scholarship. Promise to inform them of the additional scholarships to which you attach that letter of reference.
- Send a thank-you card to those who help you - guidance counsellor, principal, referees, parents, coaches, etc. Let them know how you do in your pursuit of scholarships.

SAMPLE LETTER OF REFERENCE

Dear Scholarship Selection Committee:

Please accept this as a letter of reference for _______.

I have known _______ since she began grade 10. She has been a student in my son's class since kindergarten and since grade 9 has been a member of my algebra, geotrig, physics, calculus and career education classes. _______ is an exceptionally co-operative and hardworking student. She is a patient, kind listener who has supported many classmates through difficult periods of their teenage years. Cheerfulness and a positive attitude have been her trademark throughout the years, in good times and in tough ones. _______ is a quiet student with definite plans for her future.

_______ has been most generous in devoting her time to improve the quality of life in our school. She has been a member of Students Against Drunk Driving and the Red Cross during her high-school years. She has belonged to the school choir for the last two years. _______ has belonged to the Yearbook Committee for two years and currently co-edits the School Yearbook. She takes an active part in the Graduation Planning Committee.

_______ also contributes to our town's community life despite the fact that she works part-time in the family restaurant and babysits. She has candystriped for two years, one year at St. Joseph's Hospital and currently at the Golden Twilight Lodge. During graduation fundraising activities in grade 11, _______ was involved in selling and distributing community calendars. During this activitiy, she gained an insight into the importance of service to the community and helped raise funds for the Kinsmen as well as graduation.

I am please to recommend _______ for the scholarship of her choice.

Sincerely,

Darlene Kidd
Mathematics Teacher/
Career Education Counsellor

STUDENT INVOLVEMENT CHECKLIST

1. SCHOOL INVOLVEMENT: 20__-__ 20__-___ 20 __-__

Newspaper ____

Volleyball ____

Peers ____

SRC ____

Debate Team ____

Red Cross ____

Drama ____

Yearbook ____

Choir ____

Band(s) ____

Student Aid ____

Sport (1) ____

Sport (2) ____

Sport (3) ____

Award's Night ____

Fundraising ____

Other ____

Other ____

2. COMMUNITY INVOLVEMENT:

4-H ____________________

Candystriping ____________________

Hockey ____________________

Other sports ____________________

Scouts ____________________

Air Cadets ____________________

Music ____________________

Figure Skating ____________________

Home Care ____________________

Choir (Church or Other) ____________________

Children's Liturgy/Sunday School ____________________

Employment ____________________

Coaching ____________________

Babysitting ____________________

Church Involvement ____________________

3. OTHER:

____

____

____

____

CHAPTER SIXTEEN

Your personal history

Some scholarships will ask for this, some will not. It should be part of your permanent record anyway.

Example

Position Title:	Park Attendant/Groundskeeper Macklin Lake Regional Park and Golf Course Macklin, Saskatchewan
Employer:	Martin Smith
Period:	May 1992–August 1992 May 1991–August 1991 May 1990–August 1990
Responsibilities:	customer service in golf clubhouse management of cash register maintenance of park grounds – mowing, painting, etc.

WORK HISTORY:

Position Title: ____

Employer: ____

Period: ____

Responsibilities: ____

Position Title: ____

Employer: ____

Period: ____

Responsibilities: ____

Position Title: ____

Employer: ____

Period: ____

Responsibilities: ____

ACADEMIC HISTORY

Grade 10 Marks	Grade 11 Marks	Grade 12 Marks (or mid-terms)

Include any academic awards and recognition

ADDRESSES AND TELEPHONE NUMBERS

Include home and work phone numbers and addresses of your references, your school guidance counsellor, your principal and any of your employers who you use on your scholarship application form. Also include the addresses of your high school and the post-secondary institute you are planning to attend. Other useful addresses are the department of education where you need to write to obtain a copy of your transcript of marks, as well as the scholarships and awards department of the post-secondary institute you plan to attend. Have them mail you a copy of their awards bulletin.

Example

Referee #1

Name: John Doe

Address: 1015 4th St. E.
Toronto ON M5Y 2R7

Telephone # Res (902) 955-4936 Work (789) 242-7939

Occupation: Physiotherapist

Referee #2

Name: ____

Address: ____

____

Telephone # Res ____________________ Work ____________________

Occupation: ____

School Guidance Counsellor

Name: ______________________________

Address (school address): ______________________________

____

Telephone # Work ______________

Occupation: ______________________________

Principal

Name: ______________________________

Address (school address): ______________________________

____

Telephone # Work ______________

Name of your School

Address: ______________________________

____

Telephone # ______________________________

Others:

Name: ______________________________

Address: ______________________________

____

Telephone # Res ______________ Work ______________

Name: ______________________________

Address: ______________________________

____

Telephone # Res ______________ Work ______________